# NORMANDY ON A BUDGET
## YVONNE NEWMAN

ROSTERS LTD.

**About the Author**

Yvonne Newman is an experienced traveller, lecturer and writer. After a long Diplomatic Service career serving in many posts abroad she turned to lecturing in business and written communication. She has developed her own non-fiction writing seminars and contributed to numerous publications on travel and education.

Her other title for Rosters Ltd is Brittany on a Budget, in preparation.

## Dedication

To my mother for her
constant encouragement

Published by ROSTERS LTD
23 Welbeck Street, London W1M 7PG
© Yvonne Newman
ISBN 1 85631 018 3

First Edition 1991

This book is sold subject to the conditions that it shall not, by way of trade or otherwise, be lent, re-sold, hired out or otherwise circulated without the publisher's prior consent in any form of binding or cover than that in which it is published and without a similar condition being imposed on the subsequent purchaser.

All rights reserved. No part of this book may be reproduced or transmitted by any means without prior permission.

Every care has been taken to ensure that all the information in this book is accurate. The author and publisher cannot accept any responsibility for any errors that appear or their consequences.

Designed and published by ROSTERS
Typeset by Busbys Ltd, Exeter, Devon
Printed and bound in Great Britain by
Cox and Wyman Ltd, Reading, Berks

# CONTENTS

| | | |
|---|---|---|
| Chapter One: | Welcome to Normandy | 7 |
| Chapter Two: | Normandy Crossings | 13 |
| Chapter Three: | Around Normandy | 23 |
| Chapter Four: | Gastronomic Conquests | 29 |
| Chapter Five: | Bed and Board | 37 |
| Chapter Six: | Normandy Factfile | 47 |
| Chapter Seven: | Regional Mosaic | 61 |
| Chapter Eight: | Ports of Inspiration | 75 |
| Chapter Nine: | The Road of the Abbeys | 87 |
| Chapter Ten: | Historical Normandy | 97 |
| Chapter Eleven: | Sand, Sea and D-Day | 105 |
| Chapter Twelve: | Art and Cultural Threads | 111 |
| Chapter Thirteen: | Mixing Business with Pleasure | 125 |
| Chapter Fourteen: | A Piece of Norman Soil | 131 |
| Chapter Fifteen: | Town Twinning with the UK | 141 |
| Appendix I | | 149 |

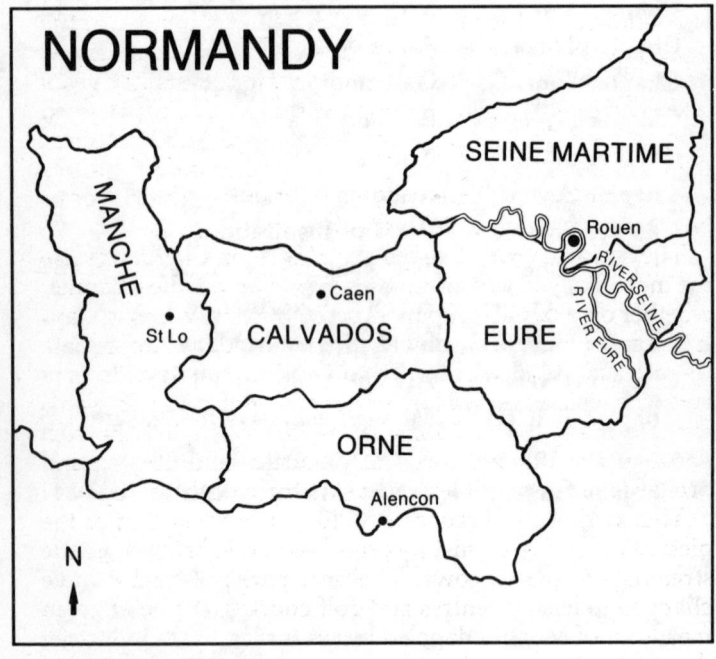

# CHAPTER ONE:
# WELCOME TO NORMANDY

One of my earliest memories of travelling in Normandy was of rounding a curve in the road and being astounded at the beauty of Mont-Saint Michel. Even more amazing is that I experience the same feelings even today, some thirty years later. Delicately poised between sea and sky and surrounded by a mysterious light, this architectural gem characterizes the whole province. Qualities of strength and power, history and culture, cuisine and enjoyment encapture the visitor to Normandy's shores and fortressed cities.

The busy ports of Dieppe, Le Havre or Cherbourg are the most likely to first greet guests from across the Channel, whether on a day's shopping expedition or for a longer stay. It is regretful that some don't stop long enough to appreciate the attractions of the nearby towns and countryside or a coastline which starts at Le Tréport and continues westwards for 375 miles to the Mont-Saint-Michel. Inland the rich pastures are famous for cheese, butter and cream, and orchards produce apples and pears for cider and liqueurs.

This 'orchard of France' is no longer entirely that of the pictures of impressionist painters—wooden bridges, gentle streams and placid cows. The neat parks of Seurat have changed to leisure centres and golf courses; the quiet green meadows of Monet's dappled leaves turned to the industrial demands of rape and sunflower seed. The scenery is not dissimilar to that of the south-west of England and the food not unlike any dairy farming district; it is the magic ingredient of Normandy that creates an exquisite flavour.

The differences give pleasure in their discovery—hidden châteaux, river valleys where anglers delight in catching salmon and trout, where deer and wild boar still roam the forests and dovecots lend a cosy extension to half-timbered houses.

Throughout the region there are reminders of Anglo connections—from 1066 when William the Conqueror invaded England leaving a graphic description on the Bayeux Tapestry, Victorians and Edwardians, rich and royal, made the Flower Coast fashionable; D-Day landings in 1944 left statues of reminder in large town and small village on the northern coast. Lately, too, there has been the exchange of friendship through 'twinning' with civic partners abroad and the growth of business opportunities in new technological expansion. Not only British visitors but other European neighbours come to look and then return to rent or buy a country gîte or a seaside holiday apartment. Some prefer the way of life and move house altogether, gaining a new dimension to their lives in experiencing another culture, milder climate, different food and fewer daily pressures.

## HOLIDAYS
As Normandy is so close to Britain, it encourages the first-time traveller, either to take an independent holiday, with or without a car, or to join an organized tour by coach, perhaps only for a weekend break. School exchanges are popular, especially between twinned towns, and young people learning French are strongly encouraged to use it—though it almost seems a national obligation to forget every word immediately after the last day at school. With the hospitality of the Normans and their ability and willingness to converse in English, this is the most effortless province for the linguistically-lacking Brits to holiday abroad yet stay close to home.

Sophistication abounds in Deauville and Trouville and there are luxury hotels in castles and châteaux, but the true Normandy is found on farms and in holiday gîtes, being woken by the proverbial cock's crow and going to market with a large wicker basket at eight in the morning, You can come back to a rustic, spacious villa, laden with local cheeses, butter, bacon, eggs, honey, pâté, baguettes and croissants and latticed apple pies—and those are just for snacks! Salt-marsh lamb has a taste sought after the world over and you are spoilt for choice with locally caught fish and sea-food. A surprise perhaps to a foreign visitor is that despite the famed French wine, in Normandy, the usual drink with a meal is cider, with the stronger apple brandy, Calvados, to prepare the taste buds for the next course during a long meal or to add to coffee afterwards.

With such a long and attractive coastline, the province is opening up to foreign and French tourism. Seaside hotels overlook long sandy beaches where, in summer, semi-naked bronzed bodies soak up the sun's penetrating rays despite any health scares or warnings. The Normandy holiday beaches are the nearest for the Parisians who invade the province, much to the disgust of the local inhabitants who have an inborn dislike of their neighbours. Foreign visitors who fly to the capital to begin their Normany tour by rail, coach or hired car to the most popular country tourist attractions—where else but Mont-Saint-Michel and Bayeaux—are more readily received.

## MONT-SAINT-MICHEL
The Mont-Saint-Michel shares the border with Brittany and although officially and administratively in Normandy, it often appears in guide books to both regions. The unique construction rises from its rocky base in the middle of a bay in which the highest tides in the world are experienced. The sea advances over 14 km at the speed of a 'galloping horse' as they say, and crashes against the ramparts of the town. It is fascinating to watch from the heights of the Mont, although not so on a rough day when walking along the causeway that leads to it. Special times to experience the spectacular tides are 36 hours after the new moon and 48 hours after the full moon, particularly in March, April, September and October. You should arrive two hours before the tide as the causeway is then under water.

It was the isolation, which lends itself so well to

meditation, that attracted the first Christians from the Western world to Mont-Saint-Michel. In the 8th century, the first chapel was built there and dedicated to the Archangel Saint-Michel. Gradually spiritual life developed on the rock as well as buildings of more and more audacious architectural styles. From the 8th to the 17th centuries, the Mont housed monks, pilgrims and the great of the kingdom.

The beauty of the spot and the reputation of the religious community of the Benedictine Order which ran the Abbey, made the Mont-Saint-Michel into the greatest centre for pilgrimages in the Western Christian world. The remains of the Abbey and the beautiful cloister are shown and described on a guided tour (in French) every 15 minutes, with two-hourly visits at 10 and 11 am and 2 and 3 pm, taking you into crypts and around flying buttresses: a truly unforgettable experience. Shorter English guided tours are at 10.30 am and 11.30 an and 1 pm, 2.30 pm, 3.30 pm, and 4.30 pm.

Always in danger of invading armies, and from its position between warring kingdoms, a defensive system was gradually built at the Mont-Saint-Michel, now the most impressive example of mediaeval military architecture still standing. Attacked a hundred times and a hundred times victorious, from the 15th century, the Mont-Saint-Michel became the symbol of national resistance and the order of the Knight of Saint-Michel became the first military order in the French kingdom.

The pilgrims and soldiers had to have somewhere to eat and sleep. It was therefore quite natural that a town should grown up at the feet of the archangel, sheltered by the ramparts. This town, the *basse-ville*, which hangs on to the side of the rock, is one of the most picturesque in France and to this day it still keeps its traditions of hospitality and a warm welcome, though stretched to its limit at the height of summer.

Walking along the sandbanks, meditating in the Abbey, contemplating the curiosities in the Museums, tasting the local cuisine, admiring the tides, sleeping in historical residences, discovering the mediaeval town, wandering through the boutiques and strolling along the outer walls, these are experiences that should not be missed. The Mont should not only be seen by day but also at night as it is spectacularly lit up. From July to September, the high-tide nights during October to June, and during festivals, it shines like a sparkling jewel, not only from the bay but from the hills around Avranches.

For more information contact: Mont-Saint-Michael Town Hall, Mont-Saint-Michel, 50116. Tel: 33 60 14 06.

# CHAPTER TWO: NORMANDY CROSSINGS

There are numerous methods of travelling to Normandy. You can go by air and sea, then on land by car, coach and rail. For the more adventurous, there's travelling by caravan or mini-bus, riding a horse, or sitting in sidecar! A good travel agent should be able to advise you, provided you point them in the right direction. It often takes some persistence to get them to recommend routes tailored to your needs rather than simply recommending what they want to sell.

Personally, I like to enjoy the travel itself as much as the holiday. When I travel by air I almost always ask if I can sit with the pilot and while I shall not be popular if I suggest that everyone goes up to the cockpit, I think probably children, young women, and travel journalists get priority. The flight to Paris or any airport in Normandy is long enough to have a look at the controls and an uninterrupted view of the Channel and the neat countryside.

## BY AIR
There are a choice of airlines and routes to Normandy, either direct or via Paris:
Aigle Azur: Gatwick to Deauville, St Gatien Airport, c/o Air France, 158 New Bond Street, London WIY 0AY. Tel: 071-499 9511.
Air Vendée: Gatwick to Rouen. c/o Air France, 158 New

Bond Street, London W1Y 0AY. Tel: 071-499 9511.
Brit Air have two daily flights to Le Havre taking just 45 minutes. Single fares start at £126, returns from £174 but there are substantial reductions for excursion and weekend visits. Company personnel who are frequent flyers can obtain 30% discount. For information in the UK, telephone Brit Air: 0293-502044; Air France (Reservations); 071-499 9511; Gatwick Handling: 0293 567175; in France; Brit Air: 98 62 10 22.

**Domestic air connections**
The French internal air service, Air Inter, carried over 16 million passengers in 1990, covering 30 major business and holiday centres. The frequent daily flights make it possible to criss-cross France in an average flight time of an hour. Air Inter is based at Paris—Orly and Paris—Charles de Gaulle airports so easy connections are made from both gateways to Nantes for Normandy. The most convenient airports for Normandy are Paris, Le Havre, Rouen, Deauville, Cherbourg and Nantes.

**BY HOVER**
Hoverspeed is the fastest rail/sea link to Paris, taking about 5½ hours, or you may cross to Boulogne to drive to Normandy. Free advance bookings are essential from a principal BR station or travel centre, or direct to Hoverspeed Reservations by post to: Hoverspeed, Maybrook House, Queens Garden, Dover CT17 9UQ. Tel: 0304 240241.

The journey is operated jointly by Hoverspeed, British Rail, and SNCF. Departures are from the reception centre on platform 8 at Victoria where you check in for a non-stop train to Dover. The 'flight' takes 40 minutes either to Calais (up to 18 flights daily) or Boulogne (6 flights daily), travelling at about 70 mph. You transfer to direct train at the Gare du Nord in Paris.

Hoverspeed also operates up to three crossings daily by the smooth-riding catamaran service, SEACAT, Portsmouth to Cherbourg, taking 2 hours 40 minutes. The Seacat is a revolutionary cross channel service introduced in 1990. It gained the record for the fastest Atlantic crossing by passenger ship before services started, demonstrating the speed of these unusual craft. They are fast—cruising at 35 knots—and spacious, with room for 80 cars and 300 passengers.

Town Twinning concessions: 9% on all published rates except for early riser day return fares. Enquiries, on appropriate headed paper, should be made to The Sales Operations Manager, Sales Administration, International Hoverport, Marine Parade, Dover, Kent, CT17 9TG. Tel: 0304 240101.


## BY CHANNEL FERRY

Brittany Ferries is particularly favoured by travellers to Normandy, perhaps because, being French, they believe their passengers' holidays should start the minute they step abroad. The famed croissant can be produced in any country but never tastes the same as the true French version, so their ships bake their own—over 90,000 a month for the company's fleet. From Poole to Cherbourg (up to 4 crossings daily) takes 4 hours 30 minutes; Portsmouth to Caen (up to 3 crossings daily) takes 6 hours.

Probably the most difficult part of planning a crossing is to be able to book on-board accommodation. The number of cabins is limited and too many people want to take the overnight crossings on a Friday or Saturday. Ferry operators generally do not start booking for cabins until the January of that year. So whether you arrange your own booking or do so through an agent, make sure you apply very early if you want cabins.

Brittany Ferries (offices), Millbay Docks, Plymouth, PL1 3EW, Tel: 0752 221321, and The Brittany Centre, Wharf Road, Portsmouth, PO2 8RW, Tel: 0705 827701. By telephone: Brittany Ferries: Portmouth 0705 827701, Poole 0202 672153, Plymouth 0752 221321, Caen 31 96 80 80, Cherbourg 33 22 38 98, Roscoff 98 29 28 29, St Malo 98 82 41 41.

Town Twinning concessions: 10% reduction on its group fares on all routes and special reductions for organizers of official exchanges. Tel: Plymouth (0752) 229418 or Portsmouth (0705) 753033.

P & O European Ferries: Portsmouth to Le Havre (up to 3 crossings daily) takes 5 hours 45 minutes, and Portsmouth to Cherbourg (up to 3 crossings daily) takes 4 hours 45 minutes. A shorter crossing (up to 6 a day) but with a longer drive to Normandy, is Dover to Boulogne, taking 1 hour 40 minutes. (Boulogne to Rouen is 177 km).

Ferries all have the same facilities: passengers may enjoy films, videos, games and slot machines, duty-free shops and bars. For details, Channel House, Channel View Road, Dover CT16 3BR. Tel: 0304 203388. In France Tel: 705 772 000.

Town Twinning concessions: 9% on published group passenger fares. Application through the Administration Department. Tel: 0304 223811.

**Shore visits**
Two popular short visits by P & O European Ferries are 'The Spirit of Normandy': Calvados Breaks, and 'Ancient Delights': a Benedictine Break.

The Calvados break costs from £112 per person on a self-drive holiday touring through the principal growing areas of Normandy. You will see the apple brandy being produced, visit the famous Père Magloire distillery where the two-stage distillation process is at work, tour the cellars and museum and then taste the finished product. As a souvenir each car is presented with a bottle of VSOP Calvados. The base is for three nights at the Hotel Friendly in Caen, where you can visit the remains of William the Conqueror's castle-house, abbey, and the nearby Memorial Museum that commemorates the second world war.

The 'Ancient Delights' car tour is a similar price, staying in the same hotel in Caen. A full tour includes the magnificent Palais de Bénédictine in Fécamp built by Alexander le Grand after his rediscovery of the ancient formula amongst family papers. It houses the distillery, museum and a treasurehouse of items connected with the original Bénédictine Abbey.

Sealink: Newhaven to Dieppe takes 4 hours 15 minutes, with a direct rail link to Rouen. There are two daily train/ferry (though Sealink call it a ship) services from London. They also sail from Weymouth to Cherbourg and from Portsmouth to Cherbourg. Head Office: Sealink, Charter House, Park Street, Ashford, Kent, TN24 8EX. Tel: 0233 47047. Tel: (Dieppe) 273 516 699.
Non-stop channel train services: these leave at convenient times throughout the day from Victoria station, connecting with Sealink ships and hovercraft to the French ports and onward train services.

Town Twinning concessions: 9% discount on published brochure and group fare prices. Requests for discounts are considered individually for negotiating trips and special visits by civic dignitaries or large groups with media cover.

All these companies offer promotional fares and inclusive holidays for short breaks and shopping trips.

## SELF DRIVE AND RAIL
The Motorail services carry cars, motorbikes and passengers overnight from Boulogne, Calais, Dieppe and Paris to all main holiday areas. From Paris, the SNCF trains will usually depart from Paris Gare Montparnásse for Granville and Paris Gare St Lazare for Cherbourg, Lisieux and Rouen but this should be checked on departure.

Motorail information and bookings may be made from French Railways, 179 Piccadilly, London W1V 0BA. Tel: 071-409 3518, Fax: 071-409 1652, and from British Rail Travel Centres and all ABTA travel agents.

The SNCF rail network will take you in fast comfortable trains (including the famous 186 mph TGVs, the fastest trains in the world) to virtually every part of the country including Normandy. To travel by train you need a ticket for the journey and a 'train' supplement for some trains running at peak hours. It is recommended that you reserve a seat, particularly on trains with supplements as they are the most crowded.

Before going on to the platform, do not forget to validate any ticket, supplement, and/or reservation if bought in France, by putting them in the ticket-puncher (composteur) separately. This is the orange automatic date-stamping machine found at the entrance to platforms. If you don't do this, your tickets will be invalid and you will be charged again and fined 75FF.

Town twinning concessions: SNCF—French Railways in London have opened a new office specializing in group travel to France. There are connecting bus services both across Paris and from the French Railways station to any final destination, all arranged by the SNCF.

For full information on French rail travel and price quotations tel: 071-499 2153 or write to: French Railways Ltd, Group Travel Section, 179 Piccadilly, London W1V 0BA.

**Sample Journeys**
*From Paris Saint-Lazare to:*
Rouen 1 hour 15 minutes through train.
Le Havre 2 hours 5 minutes through train.
Dieppe 2 hours 15 minutes through train.
Fécamp 2 hours 15 minutes changing at Bréauté-Beuzeville
Saint-Valéry-en-Caux 2 hours 40 minutes changing at Rouen.

*From Paris Nord to:*
Le Tréport 2 hours 35 minutes through train.

*From Lille to:*
Rouen, 2 hours 35 minutes through train
Le Tréport 3 hours changing at Amiens.

*From Le Mans to:*
Rouen 3 hours 10 minutes changing at Mézidon.

**Travel Calendar and Special Offers**
The SNCF publish a Travel Calendar which divides the year into blue, white and red periods. The calendar runs from 1 May to 30 April each year. The blue days offer a greater

comfort and the best prices and are usually from Saturday 12 noon to Sunday 3 pm and from Monday 12 noon to Friday 12 noon. The calendar also gives details of the various special passes or 'Carte' issued in France. To take advantage of these, it is wise to carry at least two passport sized photographs with you to save time. Most stations have photo booths, however.

The Carte Couple is a free pass and it allows a 50% reduction for the second person named on the pass when the first person buys a full ticket for a journey starting on a blue day. Couples do not have to be married and could be two persons of the same sex. Another free pass is called a Billet Séjour which gives a 25% reduction on a journey not less than 1000 km. Young people's cards, the Carré Jeune and Carte Jeune cost at present (1991) prices 165FF for a year and have 50% reductions on certain trains plus other facilities. Group Travel offers savings of up to 75% for school parties and up to 30% for parties of adults. Details from French Railways, tel: 071-493 9731.

The France Vacances Pass offers you unlimited rail travel throughout the 32,000 km mainland France network for £75 second class and £103 first class on 4 days during a period of 15 days or any 9 days during period of one month. Even if you are going on holiday for just one week you'll probably find it worthwhile buying a France Vacances Pass, either for a circular trip or for a return journey to a specific destination, leaving you the flexibility for day excursions.

France's two national carriers, Air France and French Railways, have got together to offer a bargain price ticket combining the speed of air travel with the flexibility of the train. It is proving a popular combination. The 'Flexiplan' combines any Air France flight from London Heathrow, or any of the other 15 airports in the UK and Ireland, to any of 11 airports in France via Paris to continue your travel with French Rail.

All Air France flights to Paris arrive at Air France's exclusive Terminal 2 at Paris — Charles de Gaulle Airport. There is a speedy baggage reclaim and, conveniently, it has the shortest distance from aircraft to exit of any major international airport.

With the France Vacances Pass and the Flexiplan, you can also enjoy:
— reductions on car hire at over 200 stations
— discounts in Pullman/Altea (Tel: 071-621 1962)) and Ibis/Urbis hotels Tel: 071-724 1000)
— travel concessions on the metro/buses/river trips/guided tours in Paris
— No SNCF supplements for travel in peak hours/periods nor on TGV high speed trains.

A 'Liberté' holiday combines a 'France Vacances pass' with seven or more nights' accommodation with breakfast and dinner in selected family hotels. Prices start at £279. Further information about the three special passes is available from ABTA travel agents or French Railways Ltd, 179 Piccadilly, London W1V 0BA.

## SHORT BREAK HOLIDAYS

Taking a short break out of season is usually very good value. Although the weather may not always be pleasant, people have time to converse and explain their work or customs. The Association of British Travel Agents (ABTA) made a list of Tour Operations rated the the best 'niche markets'. Some of those achieving high positions for Continental Short Breaks that operate to Normandy are:

Thomson Citybreaks
Parway House, 202-204 Finchley Road, London NW3 6XB.
Tel: 071-387 1900.

Paris Travel Service
Bridge House, Ware SG12 9DF.
Tel: 0920 467467.

Travelscene
11/15 St Anne's Road, Harrow HA1 1AS.
Tel: 081-427 4445.

Time Off
2a Chester Close, Chester Street, London SW1X 7BQ.
Tel: 071-235-8070

Sovereign
Redwing Holdings, Groundstar House, London Road, Crawley RH10 2TB.
Tel: 0293 561444.

# CHAPTER THREE: AROUND NORMANDY

Autoroutes link the major towns in the province of Normandy and Paris. These are privately owned and tolls are expensive. Unless you prefer to travel in haste you are advised to take the alternative *routes nationales* (N) or main trunk roads. There has been a recent improvement scheme and nearly all roads have been straightened and resurfaced. Off season you can drive for miles without seeing another vehicles; in summer there are numerous coaches and tourists and a high proportion of accidents, especially in Bayeaux, Mont-Saint-Michel and Rouen at the end of July and August.

**MOTORING RULES**
Certain motoring regulations differ from those of the UK and might be worth remembering. In fact, ignoring these differences could lead to hefty on-the-spot fines—or a court case.

1. No driving on a provisional licence.
2. The minimum age to drive in France is 18, not 17.
3. Seat belts must be worn by the driver and front-seat passenger
4. Under-ten-year-olds may not travel in the front (unless the car has no back seat).
5. Stop signs mean *stop*. Creeping slowly in first gear will not do. Come to a complete halt.
6. No stopping on open roads unless the car is driven right off the road.

right off the road.
7. No overtaking on the brow of a hill, or where there is a solid single centre line, or where the 'no overtaking' sign is shown.
8. A red warning triangle should be carried in case of breakdowns unless your car has hazard warning lights; these are strongly advised in any case as breakdown may effect the car's electrical system.
9. Full or dipped headlights, as in the UK, in poor visability and at night. Sidelights only when car is stationary. You must carry a complete spare bulb kit (buy before you go).
10. Beams must be adjusted for right-hand drive. Yellow-tinted headlights are not compulsory for tourist vehicles, but are advisable.

Driving in France is straightforward as long as you respect the normal rules of the road. Traffic rules are, in fact, almost the same as in Britain with the difference that in France you drive on the right and not on the left (*serrez à droite*) means keep to the right. It sounds very elementary to mention this but a friend of mine was seriously injured in a head-on accident by a foreigner driving on the right in England. Beware of forgetting momentarily you should be driving on the right, for instance, after using a one-way street, a refuelling stop, T-junction or, most difficult of all, going round a roundabout. I have driven all over the world for many years and it still feels strange going round a roundabout the 'wrong' way!

If a car satisfies the construction and useage regulations in its own country, it is acceptable in France. An international distinguishing sign (i.e. GB plates or sticker with black letters on a white oval background) should be displayed as near as is reasonable to the national registration plate at the rear of the vehicle.

You must carry with you the vehicle's registration document, a full valid national driving licence and current insurance certificate (plus a letter of authorization from the owner if the vehicle is not registered in your name).

## COACH SERVICES

There are two main coach services servicing the area. Eurolines, 52 Grosvenor Gardens, Victoria, London, SW1W 0AU. Tel: 071-730 8235 or National Express, The Coach Travel Centre, 13 Regent Street, London SW1 and at Victoria Coach Station, Buckingham Palace Road, London SW1 or local National Express and Caledonian Express agents. The daily London to Caen service starts at Birmingham and can be joined at Oxford, Reading, London, Southampton, Portsmouth and Oustreham by Service 113.

If you are planning to share a coach or minibus with a European partner during an exchange, make sure the official paperwork is in order. If you take a vehicle abroad and your hosts shares some of the seats during the programme, or if your exchange partners bring a foreign coach or minibus to Britain and your local group joins them on it, then the driver must carry a document called the International Passenger Transport Authorization (IPTA). This document is additional to the other two standard essentials—the Waybill and the Model Control Document. Usually the coach company attends to the paperwork but it is best to check that they have all three documents.

An IPTA is free but the coach company or group leader must apply for it by sending the following details to the Department of Transport, International Road Freight Office, Westgate House, Westgate Road, Newcastle-on-Tyne, NE1 1TW. The following details are required:

1. Name and address of coach operator or the owner in whose name the vehicle is registered.
2. Registration number of the vehicle.
3. Name of port of entry to UK and port of exit from UK.
4. Date of vehicle's arrival at port of entry to UK and date of vehicle's departure from UK port of exit.
5. Destination in Britain where vehicle will be based.

Any other information about the purpose of the visit, the journeys the vehicle will be doing during the programme, the passengers it will be carrying, the driver's name, etc.

could be helpful, but are not essential. Any personal enquiries can be made by telephoning Mrs M Balmer in Newcastle, Tel: 091-222 0031.

Your partner should allow six weeks to receive the completed authorization from London. The driver must have it with him/her on the vehicle before it leaves for Britain. If a British group want to take their own vehicle and share it with their partners during the programme, a similar authorization must be obtained from the Transport Ministry of the country being visited. The address will be obtainable from that country's Embassy or Tourist Office in London.

Further details about the other essential documents and regulations and conditions governing group and coach travel is explained in the publication 'Help — Guidelines on International Youth Exchange' price £5 from the Youth Exchange Centre, Seymour Mews House, Seymour Mews, London, W1H 9PE. Tel: 071-486 5101.

Other coach operators worth considering include:

Dieppe Voyages, Avenue de la République, 76370 Neuville-les-Dieppe. Tel: 35 82 31 01, Fax: 35 06 07 82, Telex: 770044. Stephen Licoys speaks good English and would be very pleased to arrange weekly trips in Normandy or other parts of France. Day tours of your choice may also be arranged: possibly to farms producing cheese, honey, foie gras or even angora rabbits. The modern, luxury coaches have English-speaking guides.

Facet Travel, Oakwood House, Eastern Road, Wivelsfield Green, Haywards Heath RH17 7QH. Tel: 0444 84351. Quality, good value tours to Normandy for groups.

Travelling Together, 44 High Street, Meldreth, Ny Royston SC8 6JU. Tel: 0763 262190.

Shearing Holidays, Myry Lane, Wigan WN3 4AG. Tel: 0942 824824.

## BUS SERVICES
There are few long-distance bus services but there are good local services. Timetables are available locally from tourist offices and coach stations.

## CAR HIRE
All the major car hire agencies operate in France an fly-drive arrangements are available through airlines and tour operators. French Railways also offer competitive trains plus car-hire rates with Avis. To give a very approximate guide to hire charges, the rental for a Renault 5 will be around 240FF per day plus 4FF per kilometre. In general, car hire is more expensive in France than in other European countries.

Most companies offer weekly rates with unlimited mileage which works out cheaper. There is a 'Super Saver' weekly rate which includes unlimited mileage, collision damage waiver, personal accident insurance, and local tax, which costs from £185 (category A small cars) to £410 (category F) and must be pre-booked in the UK with a minimum of 24 hours' notice. However, some companies require a minimum of seven clear days in order for you to qualify for the Super Saver rate.

The minimum age to hire a car is 18 years, but most international companies have raised this limit to 20 or 23 years and drivers must also have held their national licence for one year. Avis excepted, most companies have an upper age limit of 60 to 65.

**Car hire addresses:**
Avis Rent-a-Car, Hayes Gate House, 27 Uxbridge Road, Hayes, Middlesex. Tel: 081 848 8733.
Budget Rent-a-Car International Inc. Marlowes, Hemel Hempstead HP1 1LD. Tel: (free) 0800 181181.
Godfrey Davis Europcar, Bushey House, High Street, Bushey, Watford, Herts. Tel: 081 950 5050.
Hertz Rent-a-Car, Radnor House, 1272 London Road, Norbury, London SW16. Tel: 081 679 1777.

## TAXIS
Taxis are only allowed to pick up from ranks (stations de

taxi) though you may be lucky enough to stop one in the street; make sure it is a licensed taxi with a sign on top.

You should always check that cabs have a meter as cabs without meters wait outside stations and night spots to catch unwary foreigners and charge whatever they like.

The pick up charge in the provinces should be about 9.50FF plus 2.80FF per km, although prices vary from region to region. Fares are more expensive at night and on Sundays and there is an extra charge for each peice of luggage. If your ride takes you out of town, check with the driver before starting.

A tip of about 10-15% of the fare is expected.

# CHAPTER FOUR: GASTRONOMIC CONQUESTS

Normandy cooking is simple and straightforward and food is plentiful and wholesome. Butter and cream are extensively used and are served with a great many of the dishes, although this *haute cuisine* is being replaced slowly by the less rich *cuisine nouvelle*. Throughout the world the menu term 'normande' denotes a dish that contains apples or calvados, though a *sauce normande* is quite different: a fish fumet (stock) flavoured with mushrooms and thickened with egg yolk and cream.

## NORMANDY CHEESE

Four renowned cheeses come from this region: Pont-l'Eveque, Livarot, Pavé d'Auge and probably the most famous of them all, Camembert, which first made its appearance at the beginning of the last century. Today only 2% of Camembert is traditionally produced—the other 98% is made in factories all over the world.

Pont L'Eveque is one of the oldest cheeses in Normandy, known formerly as 'Augelot' then 'Angelot'. It is made from full-cream milk and cheesing begins soon after milking. The milk is given hardly any time to cool before the curds begin to form to make a cheese with a fine delicate flavour.

Livarot is a soft cheese with an even crust which has been washed and reddened to prevent mildew. It is this rose-coloured crust and round shape that sets it apart from the other cheeses from the area. It takes 60 to 100 days and five litres of milk to make one Livarot cheese weighing 600 g.

Drained, salted, and put in a drying room, it is then finished off in heated cellars with a high degree of humidity. The cheeses are put on cane or basket-work so that they do not touch the wooden slabs they are placed on while their second fermentation begins. Finally each cheese is wound with five strips of reed and is known as a 'colonel'.

Pavé d'Auge is produced in the area around Moyaux, north east of Lisieux, having been rediscovered at the end of the 1950s. It needs 5.5 litres of milk for each cheese and had almost ceased to be made commercially.

Camembert is a soft cheese with a crust with a bloom and a very light fermentation. Only 2.2 litres of milk are needed to make it and it is sold ripe after 20 to 30 days.

To make sure you are buying a real country cheese, look for 'appellation d'origine' on Livarot, a red label for real Normandy Camembert, and choose a farm-made Pont l'Eveque from Pays d'Auge.

## REGIONAL SPECIALITIES

Some specialities of the region are chitterling sausages (andouillettes) (from Vire); black sausage à la normande, or grilled, with potatoes (Mortagne); omelettes (Mont-Saint-Michel); braised tripe from Caen, or Coutances tripes in cream; Avranches white pudding, La Manche oysters, and Cherbourg damsel-fish.

Three towns, Rouen, Vire and Caen, compete for the title of Normandy's gastronomic centre. Rabbit dishes abound and here too you'll also find sole à la normande, moules à la marinière as well as canard à la rouennaise, which is duck cooked whole. From Dieppe, one speciality is marmite dieppoise—a fish stew of local sole, turbot and angler fish cooked in white wine, creamed celery, leeks, onions and fennel.

It is traditional to eat on Mont-Saint-Michel Mère Poulard omelette and leg of salt-meadow lamb. The lamb is supposed to gain its distinctive salty flavour from being grazed on the marshy coast of the Cotentin peninsula.

The local Normans all have healthy appetites and it is not unknown for some to have a plate of tripe for a snack between breakfast and lunch. Older citizens are inclined to think of fish in terms of their livelihood and prefer to eat meat. The products of the pig, so easily fed on scraps of any kind, can be seen everywhere.

Norman cuisine includes many apple desserts and pastries, all of which are varied and delicious. The fritters, custards and open tarts are often accompanied by the excellent local cream. Or you could finish a meal with sugar candy (Rouen), caramels (Isigny) and (most definitely) Bénédictine (Fécamp).

## THE SPIRIT OF NORMANDY

Cider, sweet or dry, still or sparkling, is served with everything while Calvados, the famous cider brandy, serves not only to lace or chase your after-dinner coffee but refreshes a meal, between two courses, as a 'Trou Normand'. Calvados is the traditional spirit of Normandy, distilled from cider in two stages and renowned for its glowing amber colour. After making cider from pure apple juice, pressed from an assortment of varieties of apple, it is left for two years. The juice is then drawn off and distilled a second time while the apple-cores are kept in the distilled liquid which matures gradually in hundred-year-old casks, giving a slightly 'woody' flavour.

There are no actual documentary records which tell us when Calvados was first made, but it is known that it first appeared in Normandy hundreds of years ago. It is thought that the inventor was the Lord of Gouberville, a great agronomist and gastronome who lived in the 15th century in his manor house at Mesnil-au-Val in the Manche county and who had the idea of distilling the cider he had made from his apples.

For a long time now, Norman cooks have added a glass of Calvados when preparing regional dishes and their secret is much appreciated by gourmets. I find that by beating a few spoonfuls of Calvados into thick cream cheese it gives it a light and refined taste.

Here are two of my favourite recipes:

*Lamb cutlets with Calvados caramel*
Preparation time: 15 min. (+ 10 min the day before)
Cooking time: 15 min (+ 1½ hours the day before)
Ingredients for 4 servings:
12 small lamb cutlets
2 cl Calvados
10 cl olive oil
50 g sugar
60 g butter
1 sprig of dill
1 chopped shallot
Salt, freshly ground pepper

For the lamb sauce:
Trimmings from the cutlets, 1 apple, 1 bouquet garni, 2 onions, 1 carrot, 2 tbsp olive oil, 3 cloves of garlic.

The day before, prepare the lamb stock by braising the lamb trimmings with the oil. Then add the onions, the carrot and the apple after peeling them and chopping them finely. Finally add the bouquet garni and the cloves of garlic without peeling them. Add a quarter litre water and cover and simmer for one a half hours. Pass it through a fine sieve; if necessary, reduce to 4 cl of lamb stock.

In a shallow frying pan, stir together 1 dl olive oil, 10 g butter, 50 g sugar and 2 cl Calvados. Allow to brown until it is of a light brown colour. Fry the cutlets in the caramel for one and a half minutes on each side. The secret of this recipe is to brown the cutlets without burning the sugar.

Remove the cutlets and keep warm. Pour the 4 cl of lamb stock into the frying pan and add the dill and shallot. Boil for 3 to 4 mins, adding 50 g of butter in small pieces, stirring all the time. Remove from the heat. Pour through a fine sieve and season.

Serve the cutlets on a dish with the sauce round it and accompanied by vegetables of the season.

*Grandma's apple terrine*
Preparation time: 35 mins
Cooking time: 35 mins

Ingredients for 10/12 slices:

2 kg apples
220 g caster sugar
170 g butter (unsalted)
1 tablespoon lemon juice
2 cl Calvados
4 eggs

Peel the apples, removing the cores and pips, and stew them with the Calvados. Dry the stewed apples in a warm oven for 30 minutes. Mix the sugar in thoroughly using a fork. Then add 150 g melted butter and the eggs. Mix well. Grease a dish and pour in the mixture. Cook in a bain-marie in a preheated oven (160°C, 325°F, Gas Mark 3) for 40 mins.

Serve the terrine in slices while it is still warm, with custard.

**THE GREAT ELIXIR**
The secret formula of a 'great elixir' was kept in an old leather-bound book hidden in the walls of the Bénédictine Monastery at Fécamp from the time when the monks fled the country during the French revolution. It was rediscovered by Alexandre le Grand in 1863 among his family papers when one particular manuscript of his inheritance held his attention—the reference to a natural potion created by Dom Bernardo Vincelli in 11510.

M. le Grand experimented with absolute devotion to mixing the plants and spices specified by the Bénédictine monk to perfect the 'elixir of life'. The famous spirit is now made from twenty-seven essential ingredients, of which angelica, melissa, myrrh, honey blended with nutmeg, ginger, cinnamon and cardamon are but a few.

With the unique spirit recaptured and sustained as Brother

Vincelli intended, Le Grand furthered his respect by enshrining the liqueur in a distinctive bottle, sealed with red wax.

After establishing the Distillerie Bénédictine, Le Grand created a building for producing his liqueur and also as a vault for his collection of medieval art. The result is the flamboyant, pinnacled, and highly ornate construction devised by architect Camille Albert that 120,000 visitors a year come to admire.

Bénédictine caught the imagination of its age, toasted as the favourite liqueur of the Tsars at the beginning of the century, and welcomed by the Americans in the spirit of liberty until prohibition. In Tahiti, the self-indulgent King Pomare V had a statue of the Bénédictine bottle mounted on his tombstone so that he could supposedly savour its rich bouquet for eternity!

When US liquor restrictions were lifted, it emerged as a fashionable cocktail in the late 1930s. In Manhattan—where else—a barman at the 21 Club mixed Bénédictine with cognac—a dynamic double spirit that led to a new drink sensation, the B & B liqueur.

# RESTAURANTS
## The Routiers Story
Most travellers to France know that the red and blue Les Routiers signs point the way to authentic French cuisine served in typical French surroundings and offer comfortable accommodation of guaranteed standard at a reasonable price. But do you know how it all started?

The Routiers story began over 50 years ago when a young French journalist, Francois de Saulieu, decided to travel through France in search of welcoming but inexpensive hotels with friendly service and a home-cooked meal. As a journalist, he travelled a great deal on limited wages so he decided a network of good value restaurants was needed to assist travellers. He named the hotels and restaurants Relais Routiers—*relais* meaning stopping place and *routiers* for travellers—and the company which searched for them, Les Routiers.

By 1939 he had discovered 2,000 Relais Routiers throughout France but his work stopped in the war. His idea took off again in 1945 and in 1967 two of his sons published his list in Guide Book format. The *Guide des Relais Routiers* was born, grew up, and even travelled to Britain, but travellers in Normandy can be assured that the sign still gives the same guarantee. The Routiers Guide to France may be obtained by post from Routiers, 354 Fulham Road, London SW10 9UH or bought from large bookshops.

## The Eure
The French Tourist office produces an attractive booklet, 'A table c'est l'eure!' listing over 100 recommended restaurants and their specialities.

In Evreux, oysters, salmon and duck are on the menu at La Gazette, 7 rue Saint-Sauveur. Tel: 32 33 43 40.

The Auberge du Château at Harcourt, Tel: 32 45 02 29 specializes in roast veal with cider and duck with peaches.

At Nonancourt, Le Grand Cerf, 17 rue Grande, tel: 32 58 15 27, should not be missed for its superb dishes of snails in butter, veal olives, and desserts decorated with rose petals.

## Le Havre
For a reasonably priced meal, try Les Corsaires, La Pitancerie, Le Southampton, Le Spring Summer, Les Vikings, Lamort or La Toque—all to be found around the ferry port area.

Next to the Notre Dame Cathedral is the King's Club Restaurant which serves a range of beef dishes and is famous for its upside down apple pie.

Le Monaco, a three-star restaurant, well known for its outstanding food and wine, has an English head waiter—but rest assured that the restaurant definitely offers service *à la francaise*.

In the Thiers Town Hall district, eating out is a pleasure, with menus and prices to appeal to all. The Restaurant St Pierre specializes in fish dishes; other good restaurants include Le Bearnais, La Bonne Hôtesse, Mon Auberge, Le Relais, Le Diplodocus and Le Fil à la Patte. Along the Boulevard de Strasbourg, which links the Town Hall and railway station, is Le Cardinal, a restaurant where the best in French cuisine can be sampled.

The seaside area of Le Havre, known as Nice Havrais, ends at the Dufayel Palace, which was the seat of the Belgian Government during world war one. The Palace, genteel and attractive, is an exclusive residential building with a three-star restaurant, the Nice Havrais, on the ground floor.

Other restaurants in the area that can cater for large numbers are Le Beausejour, Yves Plage, Le Plage, and Marie Christine. L'Anthanor, a restaurant for gastronomes, can also be found in the area.

More modest, but with good service, are La Brise, La Taverne Basque, La Brasserie Kanterbrau, Hôtel D'Angleterre, Le Cintra, Le Surcouf, La Manche, Le Champlain and L'Hôtel Beau Rivage and Estotem. For simple and inexpensive dishes, the Brasserie Le Week-End is ideal.

**Dieppe**
Just across from the harbour is the three-storey restaurant, Le Moderne, 21 Arcades de la Poissonnerie, tel: 35 84 66 90. It is popular with Britons on a day trip, possibly for the cheap wine and attractive view. Recommended for groups, quality has had to be sacrificed for quantity both in numbers (the restaurant seats 120) and the large portions.

Few places stay open late in Dieppe, or indeed France, but for those who need to eat when most places are closing, try Tout va Bien, 3/5 Quai Henry IV, tel: 35 84 12 67, a popular brasserie which is open every day from 11.30 am until midnight. Set menus start at 45FF or you can have something quick and cheap such as a dish of *moules* for 25FF.

Near to Varengeville, 12 kms from Dieppe, is La Terrasse (Tel: 35 85 12 54) an inexpensive restaurant in an attractive hotel set in a wood with wonderful sea views.

# CHAPTER FIVE:
# BED AND BOARD

**HOTELS**
Normandy has a wide choice of hotels, self-catering villas or gîtes, youth hostels and camp sites. One area that has expanded lately is the growth of 'bed and breakfast' facilities. These are usually to be found in private houses, advertised by a sign in the window or front garden. French hotels are graded from one- to four-star luxury. An average comfortable 2-star hotel might cost from 180FF – 300FF for a room for two with breakfast extra, unless otherwise stated, at 25-30FF per person. Most hotels expect you to take dinner when staying the night. Special rates apply if you stay three days or longer or have half-board (demi-pension). August is the most crowded month for accommodation.

The main cities and industrial centres have the large hotel chains—Novotel, Hotel Pullman and Ibis Hotels. Smaller establishments are often recommended by Logis de France: the sign of a stone fireplace with a flaming fire definitely guarantees a high standard of service and comfort in medium-priced, characteristic hotels. In Appendix I you will find a list of all the places in Normandy that have at least one hotel. This may also be used as an index to towns of reasonable size.

There are numerous medium-priced hotels, all with the basic requirements for an overnight stay. If you don't immediately find one that looks inviting make for the nearest station and you will usually find a family run *auberge* that will open their doors to you even quite late in the evening.

I will list here those recommended for the ease of obtaining rooms in high season, tolerant of your arriving at any time and with English-speaking owners.

**Le Havre**
My first port of call is usually Le Havre where I stay at the convenient Hôtel Le Richelieu, 132 Rue de Paris, 76600 Le Havre, tel: 35 42 38 71. After chancing upon it very late one night, and receiving a warm welcome from the owner (who speaks English), I have returned time and again. It is a few yards from the ferry port; the owner keeps his eye on the car in the road outside or it can be parked (with caravans or larger vehicles) in a car park behind the hotel. You can be called early and have breakfast before catching a morning ferry.

Hôtel de Bordeaux, 147 rue 1, Brindeau, tel: 35 22 69 44, is a comfortable three-star hotel near the shops but prices are a little high considering there is no restaurant or bar.

**Beuzeville**
If, however, you have time to drive about half an hour towards Honfleur, choosing the main road instead of the motorway when you have crossed Tancarville Bridge, you will come to the delightful Auberge du Cochon d'Or at Beuzeville and its sister hotel, the Petit Castel. The quiet bedrooms either look out to the garden or onto the typical Norman houses of the village. Catherine and Olivier Martin, who speak excellent English, are the hosts, while Charles Folleau and Stephane Breval prepare classical and regional dishes. Meals are served in the beamed restaurant with yellow table linen and designer arrangements of flowers. Auberge du Cochon d'Or, Place du Général de Gaulle, 27210 Beuzeville, tel: Cochon d'Or: 32 57 70 46 and Petit Castel: 32 57 76 08.

**Avranches**
Avranches offers the two-star Hôtel du Jardin des Plantes in the square of the same name (Tel: 33 58 03 68) above the Bay of Mont-Saint-Michel. Of its 20 rooms, with

beautiful views, two suites are for disabled guests. There is ample parking for cars and coaches and very pleasant and helpful staff.

## Pontorson
At a crossroads between the road to St Malo and the turn off for Les Pas and Beauvoir, on the way to Mont-Saint-Michel, is Le Sillon de Bretagne—a two-star Hotel and Restaurant at Tanis, Lieu-dit Brée, 59 rue de Couesnon, 50170 Pontorson. Tel: 33 60 13 04; Fax: 33 70 91 75. It is a delightful wayside stopping place in which to enjoy the gastronomic delights of Normandy in the beamed restaurant where seafood is a speciality. For an overnight stay, the rooms are quiet, there is ample car and coach parking, and the owners speak English.

## Mont-Saint-Michel
Hotels are more expensive than in the nearby town of Pontorson where cheap *pensions* vie with each other for trade, but visiting the Mont is an exceptional experience that can be enhanced even further by staying there, if only for a night.

Hôtel de France, 2 rue Rennes, tel: 33 60 29 17 is the most reasonable you will find.

## Fécamp
The home of Bénédictine has the welcoming and friendly Hôtel de la Poste, 4 Avenue Gambetta, 764300, tel: 35 29 55 11, in the centre of town but there is some free car parking.

## St Valery-en-Caux
In the fishing port of St Valery-en-Caux, the two-star Hôtel Altea, 14 Avenue Clemenceau, 76460, tel: 35 97 35 48, despite its imposing building, has gentle scenery over the yacht harbour. It is an excellent base of exploring the pretty villages along the coast.

**Villedieu-les-Poeles**Twenty-five kilometres from Granville and the jumping off point for Jersey, in the characteristic town of Villedieu-les-Poeles in the main square, Place des Costils, 50800, is the two-star Hôtel Le Fruitier, tel: 33 90 51 00; Fax: 33 90 51 01. In the restaurant M. and Mme. Lebargy cater for large functions of up to 150 people where they serve home-made and regional dishes. Cars may be parked in a lock-up garage and coaches have easy parking in the adjacent square.

**Honfleur**
At Honfleur, the patron, M. Leroux, of the Hôtel de la Tour, 3, quai de la Tour, 14600 tel: 31 89 21 22, will be happy to introduce you to his local golf course if you fancy a round of golf. In the centre of the town, the hotel has well-equipped rooms, a comfortable lounge but no restaurant. Closed mid-November to end of December.

**Dieppe**
In keeping with its fin-de-siècle atmosphere, the Hôtel de l'Univers, 10 Boulevard de Verdun, 76200 Dieppe, tel: 35 84 12 55, is a medium-priced charming hostelry with 28 rooms—all with traditional furniture.

Hôtel Aguado, 30 Boulevard de Verdun, tel: 35 84 27 00; Fax: 35 06 17 61, is a late 1950s hotel with its own character. It is right on the seafront, so many of the bedrooms offer a wonderful sea view. There is no restaurant, but breakfast is served in your room, which is spotlessly clean. All rooms have television with several channels, including BBC and ITV and a video channel. Rates are between 300FF—380FF for a double room. I had a pleasant stay, finding the service efficient and the staff, who speak English, helpful and friendly.

The Windsor, 18 Boulevard de Verdun, tel: 35 84 15 23 is a pleasant, old style French hotel with decent-sized rooms which somehow manage to welcome you like a long-lost friend who has become a little frayed around the edges.

A charming and pleasant place to stay is the Select, 1 rue Toustain, tel: 35 84 14 66 away from the seafront. The 1930s-style bar is an atmospheric place in which to have a drink.

On the harbour front and inexpensive, is Les Arcades, 1 et 3 Arcades de la Bourse, tel: 35 84 14 12. On the quai Duquesne, near the ferry terminal, it is a popular choice for British visitors and has a good restaurant.

**L'Aigle**
The small town of L'Aigle, in the heart of the countryside, is a perfect setting for an old-style coaching inn, the three-star Hôtel du Dauphin in the Place de la Halle, 61300, tel: 22 24 43 12. The Bernard family have run it for over sixty years and are justly proud of their Michelin star.

Hotels for Seminars and business meetings are mostly large and luxurious but if you cannot afford this or choose not to stay, you may wish to visit for a day to enjoy the sports or health centre; have a meal in the restaurant, a drink in the bar, or a walk in the grounds. Three hotels in Normandy are recommended by the organization for business and conference centres: Relais & Châteaux Seminar Guide, 9 avenue Marceau, 75116 Paris. Tel (01) 47 23 41 42; Fax: (1) 47 23 38 99.

1. Hostellerie Le Clos, 98 rue de la Ferté-Vidame, 27130 Verneuil-sur-Avre. Tel: 32 32 21 81; Fax: 32 32 21 36; Telex: 172 177 Le Clos. This is a medium-sized Norman mansion in patterned stone with a round turret and tall chimneys. It offers seminar facilities for six to twenty-five people and has a sauna and fitness room. Price: From 480FF per person, room only.
2. Château d'Audrieu, 14250 Audrieu par Tilly-sur-Seulles. Tel: 31 80 21 52, Fax: 31 80 24 73, Telex: 171 777. You might be drawn to this large hotel by its striped hot air balloon hovering above the tall trees and neatly trimmed hedges. Only 18 km from Bayeaux, Caen airport is only 15 km away, although they do have their own helicopter pad. There are facilities for up to 60 people at conferences, with smaller rooms for 20-25 people. Price: From 880FF per person, full board.
3. La Ferme Saint-Siméon, rue Adolphe-Marais, 14600 Honfleur. Tel: 31 89 23 61; Fax: 31 89 48 48; Telex: 171 031 Siméon. A large, four-storey cottage-style house set in a

garden of fruit trees. It has all the conference facilities necessary for up to 60 people, including its own cinema. For the energetic, there is an indoor heated pool, a sauna, fitness room, solarium, whirlpool and tennis court. Price: From 940FF, full board.

**SELF-CATERING VILLAS (GITES)**
A number of companies (listed below) offer self-catering holidays in a wide variety of reasonably-priced accommodation in or near small country villages. Your gîte may be a small cottage, village house, flat in the owner's house, or part of a farm. The average rent is £90 — £150 a week for a house which sleeps 4 — 6 people.

AA Motoring Holidays—gîtes, cottages, flats
Allez France—cottages, flats
Angels Travel—flats, cottages
Billington Travel—rural houses
Blakes Holidays—villas, gîtes
Bowhills—farmhouses
Brittany Ferries—flats, gîtes
Carasol Holidays—apartments
Chaper Travel—villas, farmhouses
Cosmos—coach tours
Destination France—villas, gîtes, apartments
Four Seasons—villas, flats
La France des Villages—cottages, villas, farmhouses
Frames Rickards—
French Life—cottages, chalets
Gîtes de France—gîtes
Golf Weekend—golf
Henebery—
Holt's—battlefield tours
Horse Racing Abroad—
Hoseasons—villas, gîtes
Hoverspeed—flats, villas
Interhome—flats
Intervac Home Exchange Service—
Lagrange UK—cottages

Longshot Golf Holidays—
Madron's—cycling
Meon Villas—flat, villas
Normandy Country Holidays—coastal and rural gîtes
Prime Time Holidays—cottages
Quo Vadis—villages, flats
Sealink Holidays—villas by the sea, cottages
Vacances en Campagne—châteaux, gîtes, farmhouses, some pools
Vacances France—villas
VFB Holidays—gîtes

**Calvados**
Gîtes Ruraux de France, 6 promenade de Mme-de Sévigné, 14039 Caen, tel: 31 82 71 65.

**Eure:**
Mme. I Lucas-Fayel, La Vastine, Plasnes, 27300 Bernay, tel: 32 43 21 17, has an attractive, half-timbered detached house, restored and traditionally furnished. Accommodation, which is suitable for disabled visitors, is on the ground floor, the entrance is level and doorways are wide enough for wheelchair access. Farm produce from the owner, mobile shops also call.

**Eure: super-gîtes**
A selection of outstanding gîtes may be found in the Eure, where there is space in the countryside for large properties near sporting facilities such as horse-riding, tennis, fishing and swimming.

These may be booked in English through the Service Reservation, Relais Départemental des Gîtes Ruraux de Eure, Chambre d'Agriculture, 5 rue de la Petite-Cité, BP 882, 27008 Evreaux Cedex, tel: 32 39 53 38.

Berville-en-Roumois: An attractively restored timbered house, sleeping up to ten people. Furnished rustically, it is in a former village presbytery—one room is still used occasionally for marriages. Low season, from 800FF to high season, 1500FF.

Giverville: A very similar property and price.

Saint-Philbert-sur-Risle: A large thatched house in an enclosed garden. Sleeps up to seven people. It is very near sports centres including watersports at a lake near Pont-Audemer.

## BED AND BREAKFAST

There is a growth in 'Chambres d'Hôtes' in France and nowhere more so than in Normandy. From half-timbered manor houses to simple stone cottages, all are family homes where you'll really be made to feel at home. Your hosts will provide comfortable but simple accommodation, a good continental breakfast and sometimes an evening meal too. Many are in charming country hideaways, but all are within easy reach of lots of places of interest. Rooms are clean and simple, most have en-suite bathrooms, but by no means all. The owners are very friendly and offer a warm welcome—even though few of them speak much English. Some provide an optional evening meal, usually of four or even five courses of good French provincial cooking and often including wine or home-made cider.

The Chambres d'Hôtes is part of the Gîtes de France organization which was created under the patronage of the French Ministries of Agriculture and Tourism. Like the Gîtes de France (its big sister) they all belong to the Fédération Nationale des Gîtes de France and have to meet the standards laid down in the charter of their organization.

As French people tend not to move house very often, you will discover that many of the hosts will have lived all their lives in the same house and probably their parents and grandparents too. They know where to go, what you should see, and where the best restaurants are both for value and quality.

It must be remembered that most Chambres d'Hôtes are owned by people who work—generally by small farmers and other country people. They are not professionals in the world of tourism and like everyone else, they have their own customs and habits. You will probably find they get up much earlier than you are used to and go to bed earlier too.

A selection of Chambres d'Hôtes to consider are:
**Cahagnes**
Mme. Guilbert's delightful 18th-century Norman farmhouse at Cahagnes, with oak beams, open fireplace and relaxed atmosphere. M. Guilbert makes his own cider and children can enjoy the geese and hens on the farm.

**Banville**
As a good base for the sea and to explore the beaches is another farm house at Banville, midway between Bayeaux and Caen. Mme. Lesage speaks English and children are especially welcome.

**St Leger**
On a grander scale, Mme. Clouet's ancient farm building at St Leger, near Granville, provides comfortable accommodation and evening meals in an imposing oak beamed room where the table can seat 18.

These may be booked from The Chambres d'Hôtes, 178 Piccadilly, London W1V 9DB, tel: 071-408 1343 or 071-493 3480.

# CHAPTER SIX: NORMANDY FACTFILE

**Useful addresses:**
French Consulate General
21 Cromwell Road, London SW7 2DQ, tel: 071-581 5292.
Open: Monday and Friday, 9 am – 12 noon
Tuesday-Thursday, 9 am – 12 noon and 1.30 pm – 3.30 pm

French representatives of tourism abroad:
Great Britain and Ireland:
French Government Tourist Office
178, Piccadilly, London W1V OAL. Tel: 071-491 7622.

Denmark:
Frederiksberggade 28, DK – 1459 Copenhagen K. Tel: (45)1 11 40 76.

Sweden:
Normalmstrorg 1 Av., S-111 46 Stockholm. Tel: (46)8 10 53 32.

United States:
610 Fifth Avenue Suite 222, New York NY 100 20 – 2452. Tel: (1)212 757 11 25.

Canada:
1 Dundas St West, Suite 2405, Box 8, Toronto ONT M 5 G 1 Z 3. Tel: (1)416 593 47 17.

Japan:
Landic No 2 Akasaka Building, 10-9 Akasada 2 Chome, Minato KU, Tokyo 107. Tel: (81)3. 582 69 65 to 67.


**TOURIST OFFICES**
**Seine Maritime area:**
Dieppe—B.P. 152, 76204, Dieppe Cédex. Tel: 35 84 11 77.
Le Havre—B.P. 649, 76059 Le Havre Cédex. Tel: 35 21 22 88.
Rouen—B.P. 666, 76008 Rouen Cédex. Tel: 35 71 41 77.
Criel-sur-Mer—76910. Tel: 35 50 96 65.
Ellbeuf—Chambre de Commerce, 28, rue Henry, 76500. Tel: 35 77 02 16.
Etretat—B.P. 3, 76790. Tel: 35 27 05 21.
Eu—B.P. 82, 76260 Eu. Tel: 35 86 04 68.
Fécamp—Place Bellet, 76400. Tel: 35 28 20 51.
Forges-les-Eaux—Parc Mondory, 76440. Tel: 35 90 52 10.
Neufchatel-en-Bray—6 place Notre-Dame, 76270. Tel: 35 93 22 96.
Saint-Valery-en-Caux—B.P. 24, 76460. Tel: 35 97 00 63.
Le Tréport—B.P. 27, 76470. Tel: 35 86 05 69.

**Calvados:**
Arromanches—14117 Tel: 31 22 36 45.
Bayeaux—14400 Tel: 31 92 16 26.
Cabourg—14390 Tel: 31 91 01 09.
Caen—14000 Tel: 31 86 27 65.
Deauville—14800 Tel: 31 88 21 43.
Falaise—14700 Tel: 31 90 17 26.
Honfleur—14600 Tel: 31 89 23 30.
Houlgate—14510 Tel: 31 91 06 28.
Lizieux—14100 Tel: 31 62 08 41.
Ouistreham-Riva-Bella—14150 Tel: 31 97 18 63.
Pont-l'Eveque—14130 Tel: 31 64 12 77.
Trouville—14360 Tel: 31 88 36 19.
Vire—14500 Tel: 31 68 00 05.

## INDOOR ENTERTAINMENT

### Casinos
For those who enjoy night-life, Normandy can offer 29 casinos, five of which—those at Deauville, Dieppe, Forges-Les-Eaux, Trouville and Bagnoles-del'Orne—are regarded as the best.

In Dieppe, on the boulevard Verdun, is the Casino de Dieppe which offers games rooms with roulette, blackjack, banque and baccarat. There is a bar where you can drink one of their speciality cocktails. The entry fee to the casino gaming rooms is a few francs and you will probably have to surrender your passport.

Croupiers in the sophisticated French casinos always seem to be extremely rude and belligerent. Perhaps they don't like being bothered by casual players with little money! However, the casinos are always well-decorated and pleasant places in which to relax. Don't arrive before 9 pm though or you will find yourself playing to an audience of those disdainful 'croups.'

### Theatre and cinemas
Theatre and cinema programmes or seats may be reserved locally either through a tourist office or by writing or telephoning the theatre. For music and arts festivals, write to the Festival Office, c/o the town tourist office.


## OUTDOOR SPORT AND LEISURE
### La Manche
All types of water sports: windsurfing, sailing, cruising, canoeing or diving;
Horse riding, pony trekking or jumping;
Rambling or cycling;
Tennis and golf;
Sea and river fishing;
Trips to neighbouring islands, nature rambles, meet the locals—days which enable you to steep yourself in the atmosphere of the area (its history, character and people).

Places to visit: churches, abbeys, castles, local and war museums.

### Eure

The open-air recreational and leisure centre at Léry-Poses offers beginners or enthusiasts the space and challenge of golf, wind-surfing, drifting or climbing. If you don't mind getting your feet wet, canoeing on the River Risle, for example, gives you the chance to enjoy nature and sport from a totally different angle. On dry land, Eure has a web of country paths for hikers and is home for numerous riding centres which go in for cross-country trekking.

The beautiful countryside is also an excellent setting for anglers looking to practice their favourite sport. Opportunities of hunting across the plains, marshland and forests of Eure are numerous, as are those for playing golf, with private and public courses.

There is even a touch of exoticism with the Center Parcs des Bois-Francs amusement park at Verneuil-sur-Avre, built around a tropical water paradise.

### Orne

Throughout the department there are 1,800 miles of signposted routes for walkers and horse riders with organized overnight lodgings and stabling. You can even hire a horse-drawn caravan.

Nature has also made a special effort for fishermen: more than 2,500 miles of waterways flow through the Orne department.

## POPULAR ACTIVITIES

### Walking

The starting points of short, marked walks in the Natural Park of Brotonne are at Caudebec-en-Caux and Duclair among others. There are at present ten long-distance signposted itineraries and innumerable footpaths for short or medium-length rambles. Overnight hostels can be found at many points.

There is a marked trail on the right bank of the Seine while route 23A passes in front of the abbey of Jumieges. Take the ferry to join the Brotonne Forest and the route 23 of the Seine's left bank.

**Cycling**
There are nine railway stations where cycles may be booked in advance: Bayeux, Caen, Bueil, Cernon, Granville, Pontorson, Argentan and Dieppe and Le Tréport. There are thirty or so further points where they may be hired on arrival.

The Abbey Route is 110 km and a cyclist can please him or herself, combining sport, sight-seeing and relaxation.

**Horse riding**
There are many marked equestrian itineraries: from the Forest of Roumare close to Rouen towards Tancarville, passing through the forest of Trait-Maulevrier. Numerous equestrian centres of the region are situated near the monuments of the Abbey Route. In fact over 90 riding centres offer elementary or advanced coaching, long and short ride, all-round riding contests and hurdle racing.

With its many stud farms (including two national institutions, the Haras du Pin and the Haras de St-Lo), Normandy is, without doubt, the land of the thoroughbred horse and the scene of numerous annual international horse shows and big horse-racing events, mostly either at Deauville, Caen, Lisieux, Graignes or Le Pin-au-Haras.

**Horse Racing**
Horse racing takes place at an attractive course just outside Dieppe at Rousmesnil-Bouteilles (Tel: 35 84 11 49) during August and September. The track and grandstand put some of the British courses to shame and the reason is because a percentage 'take' is deducted from each bet struck on the tote, which is a French monopoly. This means that although it is more difficult to pull off a betting coup when there is only 'pool betting', it does lead to better courses, better facilities and more prize money.

The Dieppe course is set in meadowland where racing has

taken place for more than 150 years. The track does not have the cachet or style of its coastline neighbour, Deauville, but it is a jolly place to spend an afternoon—and maybe win a few francs.

**Horse-drawn vehicle holidays**
There are four points at which vehicles may be hired, and you may choose between a barouche (a horse-drawn carriage) and a caravan.

**Water sports**
Yachting: There are over 50 yachting clubs and schools on the coast and the inland lakes.

Canoeing: Here again, there are many opportunities.

Bathing, sailing, windsurfing and water-skiing: Many safe bathing beaches and 60 open-air and 20 indoor swimming pools.

Fishing: The 9,000 miles of watercourses and 370 miles of sea coast can satisfy the ambitions of fishermen of all categories.

Underwater diving: About a dozen clubs exist.

**Sand-buggies**
These are extremely popular on the stretches of sandy beaches of the Calvados and Manche departments.

**Rock-climbing**
Suitable country for rock-climbing may be found in the Seine Valley or in the Suisse Normande area.

**Air Sports**
Fixed wing flying, gliding, delta-wing gliding and parachute jumping.

**Golf**
A total of 25 18-hole golf courses are open to the public, some 27-hole courses and many more 9-hole courses.

There are 18 hole courses at: Cabourg, Deauville (9-hole also), Le Vaudreuil, Granville, and Dieppe, Etretat, le Havre and Rouen.

There are 9-hole courses (6 in all at): Houlgate, Agon-Coutainville, Brehal, Cherbourg, Fontenay-Sur-Mer and Bagnoles-de-L'Orne.

In Calvados an annual Golfing Pass is issued for 800FF (1990), which includes 5 green fees to be used on 7 consecutive days on 5 different courses. These are: Cabourg-le-Home, Clecy, Bayeux-Omaha Beach, Saint-Gatien and Saint-Julien. For further details apply to the Calvados Tourisme, Caen.

*Public golf courses in Calvados:*

Cabourg le Home
38 av. due Président Coty, le Home Varaville 14390 Cabourg. Tel: 31 91 25 56.
18 holes — par 68. Club and house and restaurant

Public Golf
Av de l'Hippodrome, 14390 Cabourg. Tel: 31 91 70 53
9 holes + 3 — par 36.

Gold de Clécy
Manoir de Cantelou, 14570 Clecy. Tel: 31 69 72 72.
18 holes — par 72.

Golf de Caen
'Le Vallon', 14112 Bieville-Beuville. Tel: 31 94 30 25 and 31 94 72 09.
18 holes. Club house and restaurant

Omaha Beach Golf Club
14520 Port-en-Bessin-Huppain. Tel: 31 21 72 94.
27 holes. Club house and restaurant

Golf de la Ferme du Mont St-Jean
Saint-Gatien des Bois. 14130 Pont-Eveque. Tel: 31 65 19 99.
27 holes: 18 holes par 72 + 9 par 36

Golf de Saint-Julien
14130 Pont-L'Eveque. Tel: 31 64 30 30
27 holes — 18 part 72 + 9 holes. Club house and restaurant.

*Golf in the Orne:*

Golf de Belleme St Martin, Belleme.
18 holes + 3 practice holes

**PUBLIC HOLIDAYS, ANNUAL EVENTS, TRADITIONAL, RELIGIOUS, CULTURAL OR TYPICALLY LOCAL FESTIVALS**
*March*
Mortagne: Black Sausage Fair
Public holidays: Easter Sunday and Monday
*April to October*
Vascoeuil: Season of cultural activities; art exhibitions
*May*
Labour Day—1 May
VE Day—8 May
Public holiday: Ascension Day
*End of May*
Rouen: Joan of Arc Commemoration
*May—July*
Seine-Maritime Summer Festival (concerts, cultural events in historical monuments)
*May, July and September*
Pilgrimages to Mont-Saint-Michel
*May to September*
Festival of the Orne
*June*
Deauville: World Bridge Festival
Fécamp: Feast of the Trinity and Pilgrimage of the Precious Blood
*5 and 6 June*
Anniversary of the Allied Landings

*Mid-June*
Luneray European Traditional Jazz Festival
Public holidays: Whit Sunday and Monday
Honfleur: Sailors' Pilgrimage to Notre-Dame-de Gràce
Bernay: Pilgrimage with procession of the Brotherhoods of Charity
*Early June to 15 August*
Chapelle-Montligeon: Pilgrimages
*July — August*
Calvados: International Festival of Concerts
*July*
Le Havre: International Regatta
Bastille Day — 14 July. Quatorze juillet is a wonderful time to be in France. It is a mixture of Bank Holiday, street party and national rejoicing all rolled into one. Firework displays, street dancing and outdoor feasting which can go on for several days are arranged by a large committee of local people spending months in preparation. The day actually celebrates the memory of the French people who in 1789 led by the Revolutionaries, took by force the Bastille, the Royal prison on the Paris right bank where people could be detained without trial simply by a letter (lettre de cachet) bearing the King's seal. By the late afternoon of 14 July 1789, the Bastille had been seized and the prisoners, including the Man in the Iron Mask, Voltaire, and the Marquis de Sade (who wrote several of his books while imprisoned), had been symbolically freed.
*Last Sunday in July*
Camembert Festival: (Fête du Camembert)
*July — August*
Mont-Saint-Michel Music Festival
*Last Sunday in August*
Deauville: Grand Prix (Horse race)
*September*
Lessay: Ancient Holy Cross Millenary Day Fair on the moors; horse and dog fair and fun fair; barbecues
*First week in September*
Deauville: American Film Festival.

*First Sunday in September and second Sunday in October*
Le Haras-du-pin: horse-racing, parade of horse-drawn vehicles and parade of stallions.
*Last weekend in September:*
Lisieux: Feast of St Thérèse of Lisieux
Dieppe: Antiques exhibition which takes place in the casino, Boulevard de Verdun. People come from all over France to attend so it is wise to make advance bookings not only for an hotel but for restaurant meals.
*October*
Vimoutiers: Apple Fair
*November*
Dieppe: Herring Fair
Beuvron-en-Auge: Cider Fair
*11 November*
Lieurey: Herring Fair

**How to Dress**
Day wear is smart, with well-cut suits for men and women. Even on holiday you will be treated with much more respect if you dress well and are neat and tidy.

Casual clothes too are stylish, with the right type for each occasion.

Beaches: Topless sunbathing is tolerated on most beaches but naturism is restricted to certain beaches—the local tourist office will be able to tell you where these are.

**TRAVEL INFORMATION**
In 1990 there were 2,254,000 trips from France to the UK, and 6,468,000 trips from the UK to France and both figures are likely to increase by a third from 1992.

**ENTERTAINMENT**

*Radio*
There are a large number of radio stations. During the summer season the station radio, France-Inter, broadcasts news bulletins and weather and road conditions in English twice a day at 9 am and 4 pm.

*Television*
Many French hotel rooms now have television. There are six French channels and on the coastal areas of Normandy it is possible to watch the two BBC channels and ITV.

## SPECIALIST HOLIDAYS

Allez France Ltd, 27 West Street, Storrington, West Sussex RH20 4DZ. Tel: 0903 745793.

Plans 'Inn France' hotel holidays and short breaks for individualists, choosing the hotels for their setting, comfort and cuisine—some with their own vineyards.

Unicorn Holidays Ltd, Intech House, 34-35 Cam Centre, Wilbury Way, Hitchin, Herts SG4 0RL. Tel: 0462 422223.

Tailor-made holidays in châteaux and other hotels of character.

French Life Motoring Holidays, 26 Church Road, Horsforth, Leeds, LS18 5LG. Tel: 0532 390077.

Motoring Holidays in gîtes, holiday homes, mobile homes, canal cruisers and apartments or camping with total flexibility.

## MAPS
Recommended maps are:
— the Michelin Route Planning Map 911 giving motorways alternative routes, distances and journey times plus the peak periods to avoid.
— the AA Road Map of France is a clear, uncluttered map with a colour coding system; 16 miles = 1 inch.
— the Michelin Carte Touring maps Nos 54, 55 and 60 (yellow) 1 cm = 2 km.
— IGN maps, the red series N 102 and green maps N 8 and 18.

## INSURANCE
It is strongly recommended that all travellers take out travel insurance before their visit. Most travel agencies have a recommended service and other organizations that offer insurances are banks and building societies, motoring organizations and special organizations such as the Town Twinning scheme (page 141).

Students under 35 are offered cheap rates for short or very long stays by Campus Travel, 52 Grosvenor Gardens, London, SW1W 0AG, tel: 071-730 3402. Business travellers can now purchase insurance for all travel for a year, irrespective of the number of journeys.

## BUSINESS HOURS
Banks: 9 am — noon/2-4 pm weekdays and closed either Saturdays or Mondays.
Banks close early on the day before a bank holiday.
Post offices: 8 am — 7 pm weekdays, 8am — noon Saturdays.
Food shops: 7 am — 6.30/7.30 pm.
Other shops: 9 am — 6.30/7.30 pm.

Many shops close all or half-day Monday. Some food shops (particularly bakers) open Sunday mornings. Shops in small towns often close from noon to 2 pm. Most hypermarkets open until 9 or 10 pm. Monday to Saturday (many close Monday morning). The shops in the channel ports often open and close to coincide with ferry arrivals and departures.

## SUMMER TIME
French summer time starts at 2 am on the last Sunday in March and ends at 3 am on the last Sunday in September. For most of the year, therefore, France is one hour ahead of Great Britain.

## METRICATION
1 kilo (1,000 grams) = 2.2 lbs
1 litre = 1.75 pints
1 gallon = 4.54 litres
1 mile = 1.6 km (8 km = 5 miles or 10 kms = 6 miles)

1 hectare = roughly 2.5 acres.

**TELEPHONE**
France has simplified its telephone system so that there are now only two regions, Paris and the provinces. All subscribers have an eight-figure number. All Paris numbers should being with a 4, and with 3 or 6 for the Paris outskirts.

To dial France from the UK, use the international access code: 010 33 then either (1) plus the eight-figure number for Paris, or simply the eight-figure number for the provinces.

For internal calls: for Paris to Paris, or province to province, dial the eight-figure number.

For Paris ot province: dial 16 then the eight-figure number. For province to Paris, dial 16 (1) then the eight-figure number.

Most telephone booths now take phonecards and you can buy the 'telécarte' from Post Offices, tobacconists, newsagents and where advertised on telephone booths.
(50 units: 40FF); 120 units: 96FF).

Calls can be received at phone boxes where the blue bell sign is shown.

*Emergency numbers:*
Fire 18
Police 17
Operator 13
Director Enquiries 12

*To call the UK from France:*
Dial 19 and wait for the second dial tone, then dial 44 then the UK STD code (leaving out the first 0) then the local number.

Select your time for cheap rates: with 50% extra time, weekdays between 10.30 pm and 8 am; weekends starting 2 pm on Saturdays.

*How to make a call:*
1. Lift receiver and check for dial tone.

2. Insert a 5FF or 'Telécarte'
3. Dial 19
4. Wait for second dial tone (in some areas second dial tone may not be audible)
5. Dial 44
6. Dial UK STD code (leaving out the first 0)
7. Dial local number
8. Signal will indicate when to insert more coins or 'Telécarte'
9. Only unused coins are refunded.

Local international operator number: 19 (wait for tone) 33 44.

Special instructions: available from all phones including from post offices.

## POST
A postcard from France to Britain costs 2.10FF and a letter 2.30FF. You can arrange for letters to be sent for collection c/o Poste Restante, Poste Centrale, in the town you will visit. The fee is very small and you will need proof of identity.

# CHAPTER SEVEN: REGIONAL MOSAIC

The region of Normandy is divided into five *departements*: the Eure and Seine-Maritime form Upper Normandy, while Lower Normandy is comprised of Calvados, Manche and Orne. Each has its own historic characteristics. The coastline starts at Le Tréport and continues westwards to the Mont-Saint-Michel for 375 miles. Inland the rich pastures are famous for cheese, butter and cream and orchards produce apples and pears for cider, brandy and liqueurs.

## EURE
The Eure is one of the least known departements of France, despite being only an hour's drive from Paris on the A13 Normandy motorway or the RN12-13 and 14 trunk roads. The people of Eure have been farmers for centuries but lately they are changing direction towards a more urban lifestyle. The area is unique in that one third of Eure's population is under 20 years of age. Eure offers visitors numerous facilities for a get-away weekend or for longer holidays of several weeks. It is easy to enjoy the charm of its delightful hotels and its country gîtes.

Towns and villages have their own style of architecture. Flintstone Tudor-style houses in narrow cobbled streets, mediaeval halls and superb churches reflect the skills of Norman builders. There are open air markets for local farm produce; antiques to buy at auction, 'L'Eure en Fleurs' weekends to enjoy and artists in the Seine valley capturing the spirit on canvas.

**Land of history**
The east-south-east edge of Eure as it stands today was once the border separating England and France, and the site of clashes between two of the greatest mediaeval dynasties in the western world. The remains of this age of continual war are the forest and fortified towns which still line this boundary, reminding us of past sovereigns keen to consolidate their power.

One of the finest examples must be the Château-Gaillard, a fort built in less than a year (1196-7) by Richard the Lionheart. In its dramatic position high above Les Andelys, it surveyed the Seine and any threatening action from below. Only the remains of the surrounding walls give an impression of its strength, reduced to nothing on orders from Henry IV in 1603.

Eure was also the site of numerous abbeys built in the Middle Ages, some of which have disappeared; others are in ruins but many have been carefully restored. Each one played a part in the region's wealth and intellectual influence and include Bernay, Fontaine-Guérard and Mortemer.

From the 14th century onwards, noble families and servants of the Crown quickly set about acquiring estates in this fertile region close to Paris and to the King, building beautiful mansions and castles to reflect their wealth and influence.

The department spreads over the beech forest of Lyons enclosing picturesque villages where people have learned to live in close contact with nature. Winding rivers and green valleys break the monotony of recent cereal crop plateaux.

Close to the estuary of the Seine, there lies what used to be a meander in the river but Marais-Vernier is now a marshland and site of the Parc Naturel Régional de Brotonne. This park spans the Seine between Rouen and Le Havre covering 35 towns or villages and parts of four different types of countryside: the Pays de Caux, the Seine Valley, and the Roumois and Marais-Vernier areas.

Further information can be obtained from: Comité Départemental de Tourisme, 35 rue du Docteur Oursel, BP 187, 27001 Evreux Cedex, tel: 32 38 21 61.

Parc Naturel Régional de Brotonne, Maison des Métiers, Bournville, 27500 Pont-Audemer, tel: 32 57 40 41.

## SEINE MARITIME

The Seine Maritime is in the north-eastern corner of Normandy. It is a rural treat with thatched cottages, apple bloom in Springtime, dovecotes and manor houses. Along the Alabaster Coast, quiet, peaceful resorts are tucked away in little valleys, perched in the chalk white cliffs. Here you will find the large resorts which function as commercial centres and pleasure ports. The most familiar names are Dieppe and Le Havre.

Rouen, the capital of Normandy, is also the French capital for 700 half-timbered houses and much flamboyant Gothic architecture. Historic buildings include its cathedral and the equally spacious church of Saint-Ouen. Other churches are those of Joan of Arc, St Patrick and St Vivien. Rouen is famous for its 'Gros-Horloge' monumental clock archway, the Law Courts with traces of an ancient synagogue and its wealth of original museums. The river runs to the sea through a beautiful valley, described in the 'Route of the Abbeys' (Chapter Nine).

At the end of the Côte d'Albâtre, Etretat is its largest natural wonder and is also a pleasant seaside resort with an old market place, church and proximity to other places of interest: Cap d'Antifer and the 'porte d'aval' archway to the Belval needle which can be admired from the cliff-top path.

Amongst all the great seaside resorts and pleasure ports along the French coast, few can boast of a monument such as the 12th and 13th century 'Abbatiale de la Trinité' abbey church or in Fécamp an attraction like the Bénédictine distillery museum. There is a splendid view from the chapel of Notre Dame-due-Salut. The impressive line of cliffs also acts as a setting for the little resort of Yport close by.

The Brotonne Regional Park shelters 46 small towns and villages over an area of 42,000 hectares, half in the Eure and half in Seine-Maritime. Its purpose is to protect the environment and to safeguard the heritage. A signposted

'Route des Fruits' gets you into the country to see the orchards where the Seine meanders around Jumiéges. For details, contact, Parc Naturel Regional de Brotonne, 2 Rond Point Marbec, 76480, Le Trait, tel: 35 37 23 16.

Le Caux Maritime is a necklet of well-equipped small resorts, sited either at a river mouth, Quiberville, Sainte-Marguerite-sur-Mer, Saint-Aubin-sur-Mer and Veulettes, or in narrow valleys, Veules-les-Roses, Petites and Grandes Dalles Saint-Valéry-en-Caux is the central attraction, its beach and large pleasure port set far back into the town.

At the river mouth, two towns perfectly complement each other: Le Tréport, fishing port and large seaside resort at the foot of its high cliff, and the town of Eu, between sea and forest, with its château, collegiate church, and chapel. The deep valley climbs up between the Eu forest and Picardy before reaching the leafy resort of Aumale, just after Blangy-sur-Bresle. To the west of Le Tréport are two beaches at Criel-sur-Mer, counting the one at Mesnil-Val. The Yères valley road stretches from Mesnil-Val to Foucarmont.

Le Pays de Bray is a luscious green dip in the countryside, given over to dairy farming. It stretches from the Dieppe hinterland to Beauvais. The 'bocage' hedged and wooded farmland typical of all the west of France, is on the doorstep of Paris, embellished with charming small towns: two holiday resorts: Forges-les-Eaux, a spa town pleasantly situated in woodlands and with plenty of leisure amenities, and Neufchatel-en-Bray, which has given its name to one of the four great Normandy cheeses. Further south, Gournay-en-Bray is the gateway to the Ile de France and the Champagne country. On the other side of its western slopes are the two immense forests of Eawy, towards Saint-Saens and Lyons, towards La Feuillie.

Open farmland villages lost in winding lanes and the 'Cauchois' farms, surrounded by their screen of beech trees, characterize Le Pays de Caux. Hidden countryside may be discovered along footpaths or lanes for cyclists and the 'Route des Colombiers' dovecote trail. Regularly cut across by the fresh green river valleys, leading down to the sea: the Durdent, Dun, Saane and Scie, where the cider is made.

Its small capital, Yvetot, is halfway between the old oak at Allouville and the flower-decked village of Autretot.

## CALVADOS
Calvados is the home of a variety of landscapes, vast sandy beaches and green countryside which you can discover by following the signposted Cider route, the Cheese Route and the route of the Landing and Battle of Normandy.

History, architecture, pilgrimage, historical places associated with William the Conqueror, the 1944 Landings, and Saint Theresa of Lisieux, all belong to Calvados. It also possesses a wealth of inheritance: famous Norman Abbeys, cathedrals, castles, manors and a masterpiece, unique throughout the world, the Bayeux Tapestry.

Caen is the principal town of the department. Heavily bombed, it is a sprawling new town, but the ramparts, around its mediaeval castle are attractively restored round a field of grass and surrounding stream. Inside are the Fine Arts Museum witha notable collection of drawings by Dürer and Rembrandt, and the Museum of Normandy, giving the region's history. There are also the Abbaye-aux-Hommes and Abbaye-aux-Dames; churches of St Peter, St John. St michael and Notre-Dame.; Just outside the town is the Old Church of Thaon.

Oustreham has grown economically since it became a cross-channel ferry port, though it still hides beneath the name of the Calvados capital and there is little of interest for a tourist except to visit the casino or the large war museum.

Falaise is the second major town but sadly in decline economically. Instead it has taken to tourism, exploiting the story of how Duke Robert 'the Diable' of Normandy saw the tanner's daughter, Arlette, at the fountain washing linen and imposed his seignorial rights, the result being the birth of William 'the Bastard' in 1027. Celebrations of the later-named William the Conqueror are regularly held.

From being a flourishing city in the Middle Ages and later a large textile and industrial centre, Falaise was almost totally destroyed in the second world war during the Battle of the Falaise 'Gap' in 1944.

Heavily restored, there are now pleasant walks through cobblestoned alleyways along the ramparts and under the huge curbed entrances such as the 15th-century Cordeliers' Gate.

Falaise is a welcoming town, especially to its twin, Henley-on-Thames in Oxfordshire. Since they exchanged charters in 1974, residents of both towns have played host to hundreds of school children and visitors of all ages.

Lisieux is world famous for its pilgrimages to the shrine of St Thérèse. The Cathedral church of St Thérèse and Carmelite convent chapel have moved into the leisure industry with laser shows and all the paraphernalia of tourist souvenirs.

Pays d'Auge is the region which is famous for its cheese. It has many 15th- and 16th-century manor houses of weatherboarding and of timber and plaster often in chequered patterns. Following the signposted 'Cheese route' you can see the abbey church and the market hall of St Pierre sur Dives, the Manor of Harmonville; the Norman church Vieux Pont, and the Church of St Michel de Livet and its famous porch. In fact the area is quite saturated with churches.

You can also enjoy the views through the Valley of the Touques, the Forest of the Moutiers Hubert (Moutiers is an old Norman name for monks), and from the high ground at Ecots and Billot. I find the most breathtaking view is that from Berville looking over the surroundings of St Michel de Livet and the Vale of Saint Marguerite des Loges.

General Information about the region can be obtained from: Calvados Tourism, Place due Canada, 14000 Caen. Tel: 31 86 53 30; Fax: 31 79 39 41.

## MANCHE

Manche is the rectangular 330 km of coastline surrounding a variety of woodland and open country frequently coveted by others as its fortifications, towns and museums bear witness. At the Western end of Normandy, La Manche, as the French call the Channel, looks over to the English coast.

Tourism is a major way of life, offering leisure facilities, yet preserving its wealth of natural resources. Its houses, for example, are built mostly of granite, giving the region a distinctive character of its own, though not one as pretty as the half-timbered houses of other regions. Visitors can appreciate the small country churches as well as the proud cahtedral at Coutances, not to mention the magnificence of Mont-Saint-Michel. La Manche has something to offer every taste. In addition to its artistic and natural history heritage, it offers sailing, touring and sporting facilities. Local food specialities too are more than enough to satisfy anyone's appetite.

Montebourg and Sainte-Mère-Eglise overlook both the Plain, Normandy's principal cow and horse rearing area, and the access to the East Coast of the Cotentin Peninsular which was made famous by the Allied Landings of 6th June 1944. Montebourg, which was virtually destroyed, has been rebuilt around its 14th—15th century abbey church of St Jacques. Sainte-Mère-Eglise was the first French town to be liberated on 6th June 1944 by the American airborne troops. A Dakota aircraft, a glider and war souvenirs are kept in the Airborne Troopers Museum built in the shape of a parachute in memory of the American who landed on the church spire and hung there while the battle went on around him.

American troops first landed at Sainte-Marie-du-Mont on 6th June, otherwise known as the Landing of Utah Beach. On the beach are the Landings Museum and war memorials. The town also boasts a 12th-16th century church. Along the coast, Quineville is a small seaside resort and tidal port on the Sinope Estuary.

The part of the Contentin Peninsular slopes from west to east, is usually called the Val-de-Saire. As soon as you leave Tourlaville, there is a megalithic avenue at Bretteville-en-Saire and the site of the Brick Cove overlooked by a panoramic viewpoint. The small port and lighthouse at Fermanville are worth a visit, as is the picturesque Vallée des Moulins walk along a viaduct.

Barfleur, with a population of 9,000, was an important

port for the Norman dynasty in England. In the port, a bronze bucket is a reminder that the 'Mora', the Conqueror's flagship was built here. There are only 600 inhabitants today, their main livelihood is dwindling as mussel beds are being destroyed by a poisonous strain of plankton. To the north, the Gatteville Lighthouse is worth a visit and to the south of Pernelle Hill you will find yet another magnificent view.

Saint-Vaast-la-Hougue is a major oyster farming centre, with fishing port and wet dock marina, and protected by the Hougue and Tatihou defence towers. Jacques Prévert and the painter Millet both came to the Contentin Peninsula and there is no doubt that they found the surroundings a source of inspiration.

To the south of the protected coastal areas of Baubigny and Hatainville, Carteret Point overlooks the seaside resort of Barneville-Carteret, whose harbour includes yacht and fishing boat moorings. There is a regular service from here to the nearby Channel Islands.

Portbail has the same shipping links. The old town is built on the bottom of a harbour, the 'Porte des Iles' and is a resort attraction. The resorts of Denneville, St-Germain-sur-Ay, Pirou, and Gouville-sur-Mer are also at the centre of the area's mussel and oyster farming and fishing industries.

Further along the coast, Blainville-sur-Mer is similar and also has a holiday village benefitting from the proximity of the major resort of Agon-Coutainville where the holiday-maker is totally catered for. To the south of Le Havre de la Sienne, the Hauteville-sur-Mer beach extends to Mantmartin and Annoville.

The 'gateway' towns of the west coast, with the highest density of holiday homes are, north to south: Les Pieux, La Haye-du-Puits (with its interesting market on Wednesdays), Lessay and Coutances. Nearby, Blanchelande Abbey in Neufmesnil is worth a visit.

At Lessay you will find the beautifully restored 11th-century abbey church. Most of the year nothing much happens there, but every September it springs to life with the picturesque Holy Cross millenial fair. One of the most traditional events in Normandy, the fair comprises three days of fun and barbecues held on the heath.

To the north of Granville, the coast is scattered with the resorts of St-Martin-de-Bréhal, Coudeville, Bréville and Donville-les-Bains.

Granville, the fortified upper town, must be visited on foot as it is full of interesting sights. It has a health centre, the 17th-century church of Notre Dame, and 16th- and 17th-century houses. At the Ponte du Roc is a salt water aquarium, mineral museum and butterfly gardens.

The modern town stretches to the south of the Roc which also shelters a fishing port, commercial port and yacht marina. It is a lively holiday resort, especially for families, and home of the Regional Sailing Centre. It is known as the 'Monaco of the north' because of its temperate climate. There are boat trips to the Chausey Islands and Jersey.

Leaving Granville by the south, the resort of St-Pair-sur-Mer stretches as far as the Thar, where it joins Jullouville, which with Carolles and St-Michel-des-Loups, form a very popular holiday area.

Leave Carolles by the smugglers' route, via Champeaux and St-Jean-le-Thomas; you will have a panoramic view over the bay of Mont-Saint-Michel. Near la Haye-Pesnel, visit the Abbey of La Lucerne d'Outremer.

On the southern coast is Huisnes-sur-Mer, tucked away in the corner of the province, taking the coast road from Pontaubault second world war museum); it offers a breathtaking view of Mont-Saint-Michel. Pontorson, an ancient Norman stronghold, commands access to the Mont across its causeway.

Mont-Saint-Michel, the island abbey fortress, is a focus of faith, architecture, pilgrimage and tourism. Climb up the main road to the Abbey where styles spanning the 11th to 16th century can be admired in buildings. Walk up the winding traffic-free streets to the ramparts and abbey.

Outside Paris, Mont-Saint-Michel is the greatest tourist attraction in France and just shouldn't be missed but avoid to avoid crowds and see it at its best: April, May or October are the best months.

The three museums, the Grévin Museum, Historical

Museum and the Maritime Museum, retrace the stages in the construction and life of the Mont from its origin to the present day; they include many of its curios and legends.

The cathedral town of Coutances is the religious centre of the Cotentin, and should be approached from the west, along the road from Tourville. Administrative centre for the area, it is built on a long rocky spur, overlooked by the cathedral (13th—15th century) in pure Gothic style, flanked by the churches of St Pierre (15th century) and St Nicolas (13th century). Right in the centre are the beautiful public gardens with excellent views across the bocage towards the sea and the recently reconstructed museum (not to be missed). Also worth visiting: the Bishop's mediaeval park, preserved from the 11th and 12th centuries, created shortly after the year 100 by Geoffroy de Montbray, friend of William the Conqueror.

Nearby, the château of Cerisy-la-Salle (17th century) is the headquarters of an international cultural centre and the Château de Gratot has summer entertainment. Upstream of the Sienne in the Gavray region is a charming rural area with the Abbey of Hambye (12th—13th century) at its heart.

Another hilltop cathedral town is Avranches, with superb views from the magnificent flower gardens, the Jardin des Plantes, down the River Seè to Mont-Saint-Michel and the bay. The town is steeped in history: Bishop Audbert was responsible for the creation of the Mont-Saint-Michel. The King of England, Henry II, came to the little square in Avranches known as La Plate-Forme, to ask public forgiveness for the murder of St Thomas à Becket, whose relics are now in the town museum. General Patton's tanks started the offensive in Avranches in 1944. It's a lively, floral town with piped music echoing around the squares in summer. In the museum are Mont-Saint-Michel manuscripts of the 9th and 10th centuries. Visit the old craft workshops, and the treasure of the St-Gervais church; nearby you will find the Roman Church of St-Loup.

From Genets, you can get to Tombelaine and, along the beach with a guide, to the Mont. The banks of the Mont-

Saint-Michel bay provide different views from all accessible points.

At the end of the Saint-Lois and Avranchin regions, beyond Percy, Villedieu-les-Poeles is an attractive town to visit. Created in the 11th century by a Maltese order, copper has been beaten here for centuries and bells cast. You can visit the copper workshops and bell foundry and also the collection of kitchen utensils and lace museum. Nearby is the Camprépus Zoo.

Moving towards the south, near St. Pois, is the granite museum at St-Michel de-Montjoie. Near Sourdeval, the stainless steel centre, is the highest point of La Manche—Chaulieu (368 metres). A little further towards Mortain awaits the enchanting village of Bellefontaine with its leisure park.

Mortain, built on the side of a hill rising to 323 metres, overlooks the river Cance. Thanks to a hydro-electric dam the river Selune, which crosses the region, forms the twin lakes of Vezins and La Roche-qui-Boit. The river is noted for its fishing and Ducey is famous for salmon fishing.

Beyond Greville, where J.F. Millet was born, is the Port of Racine, the smallest port in France, The Hague Point lighthouse and lifeboat station at Goury, Voidries Head (120 metres above sea level) and Jobourg Head, Escalgrain Bay and Herquemoulin are points on the coast. For local slate roofs, see the Chapelle de Navqueville, the Manoir de Dur Ecu, and the village of Omonville-la-Rogue.

On the plateau, the Jobourg nuclear waste reprocessing plant, and the nuclear power station at Flamanville can be visited via the Port of Dielette. The isolated scenery is wonderful for solitary thoughts but swimming in this region cannot be recommended.

From Dielette and Goury are crossings to Alderney, Sark and Guernsey. The Siouville beach, with its salt water spa, is at the southern end of the beautiful Vauville cove, on the hill overlooking the nature reserve of Mare de Vauville and the dunes of Biville.

Carentan, the gateway to the Cotentin Peninsular, is in the centre of the marshes of the same name. It is an ancient stronghold with a 12th—15th century church. There is an important agricultural market for cattle, meat and milk products. There is now a marina in the old commercial port in a tidal basin. Carentan is also in the area of the Normandy Landing Beaches, in the middle of the American sector between Utah and Omaha beaches. The Douve and Taute basins, where the two rivers join, form a 'lowland' circle around Carentan and has a charm all of its own.

To the west (at Beaupte), marsh and marine plants are cultivated; to the south (Graignes), the trotting race track and school for jockeys enjoy a nationwide reputation. There is a racing programme all the year round.

To the south east of Cherbourg, the numerous woods are a reminder of the old Valognes Forest which used to stand between the two towns. Valognes has long been the aristocratic capital of North Cotentin and retains beautiful private mansions such as Beaumont House and Thieuville House where the Regional Cider Museum is housed in the Grand Quartier.

Bricquebec is dominated by the 11-sided keep of the 16th century feudal château, site of an ancient mediaeval stronghold. Inside the château is the Regional Ethnographic Museum.

The Vire crosses the Saint Lois Bocage from south to north. At Saint-Lô, the heart of the Manche, it flows at the foot of the fortified rock 'The Enclos', the site of the ancient city. The town is now, built on and around the rocky spur on which the original ramparts were built after being almost totally destroyed in 1944. Its title in 1944 was the 'Capital of the Ruins' during the battle for its liberation. It is now an ideal touring centre for the rest of the Manche. The Fine Arts Museum is in the new modern Cultural Centre.

Take time to visit the National Stud, where stallions are kept for the breeding of racehorses, trotters and Percherons. Teams of horses are on show on Thursdays during the summer (mid July to the beginning of September) and there is a lively market on Saturdays. Around St-Lô there are dairy product factories at Pont-Hebert and Condé-sur-Vire. Near Tessy is the site of the Vire Chapel and Langotière Château in Domjean.

## ORNE

The Orne department seems to have signed a pact with the forces of nature, offering hospitality, silence and respect for others. Forests have been tamed, orchards planted, alliances made with health-giving springs, and river beds left untouched. There are no large towns or cities in this country area of wood and pasture although tourist offices can be found at L'Aigle, Alençon, Athis, Bagnoles-de-l'Orne, Bellême, Champsecret, Dompierre, La Ferrière-aux-Etangs, La Chapelle-Montligeon, Domfront, Essai, La Ferté-Mace, Gacé, Mortagne-au-Perche, Putanges-pont Ecrepin, Ranes, Sées and Vimoutiers.

Bellême, twinned with Goring-on-Thames in Oxfordshire, arranges successful twin exchanges with cyclists and other sports enthusiasts, even taking in their stride more than their fair share of occasional accidents and illness.

The cultural activities of the Orne department concern themselves with the restoration of old monuments and châteaux; they arrange a season of concerts and recitals each year and encourage arts and crafts as part of the tradition of the region. A symbol of this is Alençon lace: 'The Queen of laces, fit for the Queen.' Further information about the Orne may be obtained from: The Comité Départemental du Tourisme, 88 rue Saint-Blaise, BP 50, 61002 Alencon Cedex. Tel: 33 28 88 71.

# CHAPTER EIGHT:
# PORTS OF INSPIRATION

**DIEPPE**
Dieppe grew up round the mouth of the river Arques from which, in the 11th century, the Vikings gave it the name 'diep' meaning deep rivers. After the Battle of Hastings, the town became a prosperous port for Franco—British trade. During the 14th- and 15th centuries it was renowned as a seafaring town and by the early part of the 16th century its prosperity showed in its display of new public buildings, stone quays and the churches of St Remy and St Jacques. At the same time, Jehan Ango, a wealthy shipbuilder and counsellor, built a fleet of ships which sailed to all parts of the world. Ango built a palatial wooden residence in Dieppe where he entertained lavishly—particularly King François I, who made him Viscount of Dieppe. Disaster struck in 1694 when the British and Dutch fleets burned the mediaeval town, which was known as the City of Carved Oak. Only the churches of St Remy, St Jacques and the castle remained. A new town of brick and stone had to be built.

In the early 1800s, the British this time peacefully 'invaded' Dieppe. The natural light of the area, the coastline and surrounding countryside attracted a number of English painters and authors such as Cotman and Turner while later it became the favourite haunt of Walter Sickert and Whistler. Oscar Wilde wrote The Ballad of Reading Gaol while exiled in Dieppe. Many French artists also enjoyed the charms of the town, notably Carot, Monet, Pissaro, Renoir and Degas.

The strange enthusiasm of English visitors for bathing in

the sea sealed the success of Dieppe. Special hot sea water baths were popular and a casino and theatre became added attractions. The town became a fashionable seaside resort. The sea front with impressive views of the Alabaster Coast, a 59-mile stretch from Dieppe to Etretat, might still keep its air of nostalgia with Edwardian hotels named Windsor and Epsom but today Dieppe is an important port with international passenger and freight links. The fishing port is around the area where the Newhaven ferry docks; it is a naval centre and commercial port handling catches of fish and products from the Antilles—mostly bananas.

**Canadian connections**
In the 15th century, Jehan Ango's fleet landed in Newfoundland and developed trade links, while Dieppe pioneers founded Quebec and played a large part in establishing the French colonies in Canada. The link was further sustained in the second world war with Operation Jubilee on 19 August 1942. This was the first Allied reconnaissance of the European coast when 7,000 men, mostly Canadians, landed at eight different points between Sainte Marguerite to the west and Berneval to the east but the only German strong-point to be taken was the battery near the Ailly lighthouse. Under heavy fire, more than 5,000 men were killed or taken prisoner in a short and bloody battle which many people feel should never have taken place. It was later justified by the Allied Command as a preliminary test before the 1944 Normandy invasion. The Canadian influence today is perpetuated in Dieppe with flags, memorials and place names, such as Square du Canada and Avenue des Canadiens.

**Visiting the town**
Dieppe is an important tourist centre offering a variety of sights, hotels and restaurants, a reasonable, if pebbly beach, and a large selection of sports and leisure activities. The sea front has been remodelled since the last war, and a new town hall, parks and pedestrian precincts constructed.

*Le bout de quai* is a network of narrow streets, some of them dark and sombre, between the quay and the beach. Statues of the Virgin Mary built into the walls of the buildings high up near the roof, give thanks for saving their owners from the plague.

Le Pollet is on the left as you enter the port and was originally the fishermen's quarter. Using a range of steps the energetic can climb to the top of the cliffs and gain a marvellous view over the whole of Dieppe and the surrounding area.

The 15th-century castle, the 'old château' which dominates the port from the west, is faced with flint and sandstone and was built round a huge circular tower which was part of the earlier 13th-century town fortifications. There were some additions in the 16th and 17th centuries and in the 18th century the castle walls were reinforced.

Using the drawbridge, you can visit the castle museum (open every day from 10 am to 12 noon and 2 pm to 6 pm. Closed Tuesdays out of season). Exhibits include early ships' models, old maps and navigation instruments, pre-Colombian pottery, and a unqiue collection of carved ivory. The Dieppe Ivories were not designed to be purely decorative but objects such as incense boxes or compasses had a more practical use. In the 17th century there were 350 ivory carvers who fashioned the ivory imported by 'explorers' from Africa. Some of the best examples in the world are on show in the museum.

There are also paintings of local scenes by Isabey, Boudin, Pisarro and other 19th-century artists. The collection of prints by one of the originators of cubism, George Braque, who lived in Dieppe, is too large for permanent display but may be seen on request.

St-Jacques' Church is a rich, pure Gothic building with parts dating from the 13th century. The 15th-century tower has a very pretty rose window. Some of the voyages of the Dieppe explorers are described on a frieze in the church. Not so impressive as St Jacques, the Church of St Remy has, however, a huge organ dating back to 1740 which is one of the most beautiful in France.

## Shopping

One of the pleasures of shopping in Dieppe is that the great variety of shops are all close together. Most of the main shopping streets fan out from the Place due Puits Salé (the place of the salty wells!) which is also where you will find one of the landmarks of Dieppe—the Café Les Tribuneaux, a loud, dark, smoky and overcrowded bar.

The wonderful fish market on the corner of Quai Duquesne (named after Louis XIV's Admiral, Abraham Duquesne, who was born in Dieppe in 1610) displays the wide choice of fresh fish and shellfish that can be found only in a port.

Along the Grande Rue, a pedestrian walkway, are two department stores, Printemps and Prisunic, while for fashionable shoes and handbags, Divergence at 129 keeps to reasonable prices. Yves St Brice sells hair accessories, attractive earrings and watches. Kitchen and glassware may be found at Geneviève Lethus and next door to her, especially for art deco lamps and pewters, is Antiquities. At 113, Ratel supplies home-made chocolates of mouth-watering delight—I can never resist taking some home, beautifully packaged and tied with gold ribbon.

On Saturday mornings the whole the centre of Dieppe becomes one large open air market place (with a smaller market on Tuesdays and Thursdays). Fruit, vegetables, flowers, meat, game, fish, groceries, cheese, clothes, toys, hardware and much more. You will find stall after stall around Rue St Jacques, filling the whole of the Place Nationale and the length of the Grande Rue.

Outside the town, on the RN27 towards Rouen at the Val Druel Centre Commercial, is the Mammouth Hypermarket. Absolutely huge, there is a wide selection of everyday goods—French style.

If you are giving yourself up to a day's shopping, the Miami restaurant at the Centre is recommended for a cheap self-service meal after the exertions of trolley pushing. The other large supermarket, Intermarché, is on the outskirts of Dieppe in the industrial zone. Both are closed on Sundays.

**Local information**
The Tourist Office is in Boulevard Général de Gaulle. Tel: 35 84 11 77.
Railways station (SNCF): TEl: 35 84 20 71.
Taxis: Tel: 35 84 20 05.
Airport (light aircraft only): Tel: 35 84 14 40.
Police (non-emergency): Tel: 35 84 87 32.

**VARENGEVILLE-SUR-MER**
The Ailly Lighthouse is at Varengeville-sur-Mer, a seaside resort with a number of half-timbered houses in a beautiful setting, about 12 miles west of Dieppe. The lighthouse is open from April to September from 9 am to 12 noon and 2 pm to 6 pm. It is worth a short detour from the village if you would like to enjoy the wonderful 40-miles view along the cliffs from the lighthouse upper platform. Many painters have been attracted to this area and George Braque is buried in a churchyard here,

Anyone interested in gardens should not miss a visit to Le Bois des Moutiers House and its garden, a lovely estate with an extensive collection of rare trees and shrubs and masses of beautiful flowers. The house was designed by the English architect Sir Edward Lutyens and is the only one in France in this style. It dates from the 1898 and is one of the best examples of his early work. The interior and furnishings are examples of the arts and crafts movement and there is a fine tapestry designed by Burne-Jones on the main staircase.

Lutyens created the house for Madame Guillaume Mallet, an American, around her twin passions for gardens and music. In the front of the house is the formal garden, while the long windows of the music room look out on the natural park and are a perfect complement to the house. The house is open only in the summer from 10 am to 12 noon and 2 pm to 7 pm. The garden is open from 15 March to 14 November, except Sunday mornings.

**LE HAVRE**
Twinned with Southampton and Leningrad, Le Havre stands

at the estuary of the River Seine, 140 miles north west of Paris and 53 miles west of Rouen. Over a million visitors arrive from Great Britain every year, though many only pass through the ferry terminal on their way to other parts of France and Europe. Although the town has adopted a welcoming logo 'Bonjour Le Havre' to encourage them to stay— few do so for more than one night.

Le Havre (The Harbour) was only a fishing village with a chapel dedicated to Notre Dame de Grâce until in 1516 it was named by King François I as Le Havre de Grâce as he began the building of the port to replace Honfleur and Barfleur. In 1562 the town was handed over to the keeping of Queen Elizabeth I by Louis I, Prince of Condé and leader of the Huguenots, but the English, led by the Earl of Warwick were driven out the following year by Charles IX. Defences and harbour works were continued under Cardinal Richelieu and completed by the engineer, S le P de Vauban.

Le Havre was a port of considerable importance as early as 1572 and sent ships to the cod and whale fishing grounds off Norway and Canada. Napoleon made it into a great naval harbour, and building and development works were continued by Napoleon III. During the first world war, Great Britain and the United States used Le Havre to land stores and troops, and after the fall of Antwerp and Ostend, and the seat of the Belgian government was transferred there.

During the second world war, the town suffered extensive damage during more than 170 bombing raids. Seven out of eight buildings were completely destroyed and the eighth usually damaged. Le Havre was captured by the Germans in June 1940 and liberated in September 1944. The Musée de l'Ancien Havre, in one of the historic buildings that escaped the bombing, is at 1 rue Jérome-Bellarmato at the end of the Quai de Southampton. It has pictures and mementoes of the Old Havre from pre-war days, beautiful 18th-century maps, Chinese porcelain, and models of sailing ships. Open: 10 am to 12 noon and 2 pm to 6 pm, closed Monday and Tuesday. Entrance free. Tel: 35 42 27 90.

In 1945, the French Government appointed the architect August Perret (1874-1954), to design the new town and the reconstruction of Le Havre to his plan continued to 1964. Although there is an air of greyness, particularly in the winter when there are no flowers on the balconies, Perret made good use of space, with wide avenues and large squares. He also blended the few remaining old buildings sympathetically into the surroundings. Just when you think a street is beginning to be monotonous you come across a small church or turn a corner that opens onto a large grassy square playing host to an impressive modern statue.

Le Havre now boasts seventy-one restaurants, numerous cafes, wine shops and sports facilities. The country's second seaport after Marseilles, it is renowned for its surf-boarding centre and a 1,300-berth yachting marina open 24 hours a day. Tel: 35 21 23 95.

Overlooking the port between the beach and the marina is Le Havre's ocean gate, the Porte Oceane, two 14-storey buildings erected at the eastern end of Avenue Foch, and which are wider than the Champs Elysée in Paris.

One of the most impressive buildings in a large square in the new town of Le Havre between the far end of Avenue Foch as it runs east to west from the sea and the Boulevard de Strasbourg with its fine shops and restaurants, is the Town Hall, *l'Hôtel de Ville*. Here the receptionists continue to be surprised at the number of English people who try to book rooms there! They are directed to the Tourist Information Office in the same building.

Walking to the left from the Town Hall along Avenue Réné Coty into the heart of the Thiers district, you will find Le Havre's unique link between the lower and upper halves of the town—the funicular railway, open every day except Sundays and bank holidays. This is the easy way of reaching the part of the town on the high chalk cliffs, which is an ideal point for obtaining spectacular views across the town and the mouth of the Seine. Halfway between the upper and lower towns is St Michel's Chapel (Chapelle St Michel), the original 13th-century church of Ingouville, the village which was in existence before François designed Le Havre's port.

Turning left when you leave the ferry terminal, you can enjoy a traffic-free walk for miles along Le Havre's coastline with only the seagulls' noisy accompaniment. You first pass the Port Signal Station tower and about 1,000 yards away are two safe anchorages for motor boats.

Across the road in Boulevard J F Kennedy is the grey stone Musée des Beaux Arts (Museum of Fine Arts), built in 1958. The Andrew Malraux Art Gallery has a delightful collection of Impressionist paintings as well as examples of unique glass and porcelain. The glass entrance doors, up a ramp over a shallow moat, have a delicate sculpture below representing the knitting implement used by fishermen to repair their nets.

Eugène Boudin (1824−98), who worked as a picture-framer in Le Havre, has fifty canvasses at the museum, though not all of them hung. The Dutch painter Terbruggen, De Keyser and Van de Velde provide perspectives of people and the sea, while local town views by Pisarro, Monet's *Westminster Abbey*, and examples of Raoul Dufy's work make the museum well worth a visit. Le Havre was Dufy's (1877−1953) home town and the room where his paintings are displayed is attractively designed to extend through floor level picture windows to the waterlilies on a moat outside.

The opening hours, which unfortunately do not conveniently coincide with the arrival or departure of cross-channel ferries, are 10 am to 12 noon and 2 pm to 6 pm, closed Tuesdays. Entrance is free but you must collect a ticket from the reception desk on arrival. You are asked not to touch the exhibits—if you do, an awful noise echoes through the spacious halls!

Continuing along the edge of the sea, this attractive district of Le Havre begins at St Rosh Gardens and stretches for 1.5 miles to Sainte-Adresse and the Nice Havrais—named after the city of Nice—where, on the higher ground, are some of the most desirable properties in Le Havre. Near the Dufayel Palace is the Notre Dame des Flots Chapel, a place of pilgrimage for sailors.

Used by fishermen as a navigational aid before the lighthouse was built at Le Havre, the Sugar Loaf—le Pain de Sucre—is unmistakeable. It is painted white, and is conical in shape. On its walls is a plaque recalling that it was built in memory of General Levevre Desnouette who was drowned off the coast of Ireland in 1832. On summer weekends, this beach area, sandy and pebbly, is immensely popular, and very crowded with sunbathers and swimmers.

**Shopping**
Many British visitors come for a day's shopping and a good place to start and finish is Rue de Paris—a few yards from the ferry terminal. You can start at Les Halles, a covered market close to the Musée des Beaux Arts in Boulevard Kennedy. The cluster of little shops include Cheinisse, where there are always more than 100 varieties of cheese available. The staff will advise you on which cheese is best for the time of year.

Making your way back to the Rue de Paris, where the only building left standing after the war was the Notre Dame Cathedral, the Nouvelles Galleries has two floors of goods ranging from the luxury to the essential. Continuing to walk away from the sea and off to your right is the grand new Bassin de Commerce with glass-fronted buildings and the tall tower of the *Espace Oscar Niemeyer*—a showpiece cultural centre with a theatre, cinema, restaurants, bars and shops. You may decide to go no further, but there is still much more to see.

At the Place de l'Hôtel de Ville are quality leatherware shops and perfumeries and on Avenue Réné Coty is Printemps, a small version of the large Paris store, where you can see the latest in French fashion. Evening wear and coats are particularly good buys, for both price and style. Across the road is Bruneau-Roche, one of the many small shops in Le Havre making and selling its own delicious chocolates. A few yards along the road is Monoprix, a large store that sells practically everything at down-to-earth prices.

You could round off the days with a contrast—a ride on a number 71 bus to Mont-Gaillard to visit the Auchan hypermarket where fifty shops make this complex one of the most attractive in northern France. As a word of caution, unless that have changed their policy recently, Auchan will only accept cash or the Visa card in Le Havre. At the hypermarket you will need a ten franc or two franc piece to put in the machine to get a trolley from the car park. The money is returned when you replace the trolley. Hypermarkets and supermarkets rarely shut for lunch and are usually open until nine or ten in the evening. There are plenty of taxis for your return trip to the ferry or the Rue de Paris.

**Local information**
Cinema: Le Colisée, 154 Bd de Strasbourg, Tel: 35 22 86 88.
International Seamen's Hospital. Tel: 35 24 51 61.
Church of England, 58 Rue Lord Kitchener, Holy Trinity Church, services: third Sunday of each month.

Local transport: No 7 to Halles Centrales (covered market) and Mont-Gaillard (Hypermarket) through L'Hôtel de Ville. No 11 Hôtel de Ville (Town Hall/Mont-Gaillard (Hypermarket) via the Gare (railway).

Tourist Information: Ferry Terminal, quai de Southampton 76600 Le Havre. An office with very helpful English-speaking staff will give you maps, lists of hotels and any local information you may require as you leave or arrive at the terminal.

Tourist Office: Forum de l'Hôtel de Ville, BP 649, 76059 Le Havre Cedex. Tel: 35 21 22 88. Open: 9 am to 12 noon and 2 pm to 7 pm weekdays.

## CHERBOURG
At the top of the Cotentin commanding the peninsular between La Hague and the Val-de-Saire, the bustling port of Cherbourg and its neighbouring villages comprise a community of more than 100,000 inhabitants but although Cherbourg has all the leisure facilities of a lively town, it will mainly only attract those connected with commercial marine life or sailing.
 Cherbourg's military port is crowded with naval ships and it is also a nuclear submarine construction base. As a cross-channel and commercial port there are car ferries to England and Ireland and freightliners to the Channel Islands. It is

also a passenger port for transatlantic liners such as the QE2. The port of Cherbourg is entirely artificial in the sense that it was man-made in an otherwise poorly sheltered location. Work began in the 18th century and continued through the 19th and even into modern times where many acres of land have been reclaimed from the sea.

Napoleon was instrumental in the development of the port and a bronze equestrian statue of him by Armand Le Veel (1821−1905) looks out over the harbour from the flower beds in Place Napoléon. His Fort du Roule, built on a rocky promontory 367 feet overlooking the town, now houses the War and Liberation Museum which can be reached by following the *Circuit du Débarquement* sign to the right on entering Cherbourg on the N13. The Museum map room follows the progress of the Allied Landings in Normandy and in an adjoining room the capture of Cherbourg on 27 June 1944 is illustrated graphically. There is also an interesting collection of German and British propaganda material—newspapers, pamphlets and posters.

The museum has had several recent burglaries so some exhibits are sadly depleted, including French war medals in which I was particularly interested since my uncle had received the Croix de Guerre: an honour indeed, and one rarely, if ever before, given to a British soldier.

Art lovers are catered for at the Thomas Henry Museum in the purpose-built cultural centre where Fra Angelico's altarpiece *The Conversion of St Augustine*, and Filippo Lippi's *Entombment* are two of many early works to be appreciated. The museum has a substantial number of portraits by the local artist Jean-François Millet (1814−75).

The Prehistoric and Ethnographic Museum is at Parc Emmanuel Liais, named after the naturalist and astronomer Emmanuel Laias (1826−1900) who designed the tropical plant garden. The museum has unusual exhibits of the lives of Eskimos, with seal-skins kayaks and dog-sledges with whale bone runners.

**Shopping**
Many day visitors simply drive to the hypermarket on the

outskirts, and often miss the delights of shopping in the centre. Apart from interesting shops, there's a market in the Place de Gaulle on Thursdays and a colourful flower and vegetable market on Tuesday.

**Tourist information**
Tourist Office: 2 quai Alexandre, near the Avant Port, tel: 33 53 30 11. Helpful staff will give you a local map, a list of events held in the summer, and make hotel bookings.

# CHAPTER NINE:
# THE ROAD OF THE ABBEYS

One of the major tourist routes planned by the Upper Normandy Tourist Authority is the Road of the Abbeys, which follows the Valley of the River Seine, passed churches, châteaux and museums, in a landscape setting of alternating chalk cliffs wooded slopes and forest. Although the official route begins at Rouen, I usually start the journey from Le Havre.

Ocean liners on the winding reaches of the Seine as far as Rouen come as a shock as they glide past the fields and villages while passengers intrude into the scenery on steamer cruises as they admire historical sites and monuments from the water. This lazy meandering may be enjoyed on The Salamandre runs from the Quay at the Marina, Le Havre (Tel: 35 42 01 31).

The banks of the Seine are joined in two places by the famous Brotonne bridge and the Tancarville bridge while eight ferries play back and forth daily.

**Graville Priory at Le Havre**
The Priory Church of Graville (Prieuré de Graville) was built during the second half of the 11th century but has been altered over the centuries. During the 13th century the choir and the side-aisles were re-constructed and the convent and cloister were added. The museum combines a sociological record of old Le Havre, with paintings, old photographs, and sketches.

There is also an important collection of religious art and

150 models of fine houses of the 12th to the 17th century known as the 'Gosselin collection'. These models of old Norman and Breton houses fill several rooms and fascinate visitors of all ages.

Every Friday during the summer there is an evening of folk music and theatre to which entry is free. Also, in the 159-seat auditorium, chamber concerts and recitals are held. Another attraction is the French equivalent of a mediaeval banquet.

The Priory is open from Wednesday to Sunday except 1 January, 1 May, 8 May, 14 July, 11 November, 25 December, from 10 am – 12 pm and from 2 pm – 6 pm. Free. It can be reached by a No 2 bus. Tel: 35 47 14 01.

### The Abbey Church Saint-Sauveur at Montvilliers

Thirteen kilometres north-east of Le Havre an Abbey for women was founded in the 6th century by Saint Philibert and gave its name to Montivilliers which means 'monastery estate'. In the Roman church, built in the 11th century, admire the two arms of the transept topped by a lantern tower. The nave was granted to the parish in 1241 and enlarged in the 16th century by the addition of a lateral gothic nave. The abbey buildings situated nearby are in the process of being restored.

Open from 8 am – 12 pm and from 2 pm – 5 pm except on Sunday afternoon. Can be reached by a No. 9 or No. 12 bus from Le Havre.

### Priory Museum at Harfleur

Harfleur is six kilometres east of Le Havre and was a huge port until it silted up in the 16th century. The spire of the Church of Saint Martin can be seen for miles. The Priory Museum has been set up in a 15th-century half-timbered hospice which welcomed navigators on a stopover at Harfleur. Three rooms successively represent the occupation of the site of Harfleur during prehistoric times and modern times. In another room the pre-eminence of the church is demonstrated by models and engravings.

Open from Wednesday to Saturday including from 3

pm — 6 pm and Sundays from 10 am — 12 pm and from 3 pm — 6 pm. Closed on public holidays. Entrance fee: groups of more than ten persons are free. Tel: 35 45 40 62.

**The Château of Orcher at Gonfreville l'Orcher**
A fortress, with elegant interior decor, which was rebuilt in the 18th century is situated at the highest point of the cliff and minates the Seine estuary. It has a vast wooded park designed in the 18th century which borders a terrace 600 metres long and from where the view is superb.

The park is open every day from 9am — 5 pm except on Thursdays. The château is open from 3 July — 15 August daily. Entrance fee: groups by appointment at reduced price. Tel. 35 45 45 91.

**The Castle of Filières, (Château de Filières) Gommerville**
Only the left wing remains of the small castle built under Henry IV, the major part of the building having been rebuilt in the 18th century. The rooms on the ground-floor, including the Chinese sitting room, have sculptures by Ingres the Father, furniture, period paintings and 16th and 17th century books, as well as art objects from all corners of the world.

Open daily from 14 July to 20 August, and Wednesday, Saturday, Sunday and Bank Holiday afternoons between Easter and All Saints Day. Tel: 35 20 53 30.

**Gruchet-le-Valasse: The Abbey of Valasse**
The Cistercian abbey was founded by Waeran de Meulan and the Empress Mathilda, grand-daughter of William the Conqueror. Here the memory of Thomas à Becket, Archbishop of Canterbury, is recalled. Fine rooms in early Gothic style with magnificent Norman capitals which have withstood successive transformations. The abbey church disappeared after the departure of the monks during the French Revolution; the present day abbey has a very beautiful classical facade. Exhibitions, conferences and symposiums are held there.

Guided visits on the second and fourth Sundays during

April to November, 2.30 pm – 5.30 pm. Entrance fee: groups by appointment at reduced prices. Tel: 35 31 03 02.

### The Museum of Popular Arts and Traditions, (Musée des Arts et Traditions Populaires) Lillebonne

The museum holds Gallo-Roman collections; collections of interesting and local history from the 18th and 19th century; chinaware, art objects, furniture and documents.

Open from 1 May to 30 September daily from 2.30 pm – 6.30 pm except Tuesday. Open from 1 October to 30 April, Saturday, Sunday and public holidays from 2.30 pm – 6.30 pm. Entrance fee: groups at reduced price. Tel: 35 38 53 73.

### The Church of Mesnil-sous-Lillebonne

An exceptional collection of minerals and fossils found essentially in the Pays de Caux are exhibited in a church dedicated to Saint Anne, constructed in the 12th century and continued in the 16th century. The reredos of the main altar of the church, entirely restored, comes from the chapel of Saints-Ange which was destroyed after the French Revolution.

Open daily from 1 May to 30 September, 2.30 pm – 6.30 pm except Tuesday. Commentated visits for school children. Entrance fee: groups at reduced price. Tel: 35 38 30 52.

### Lillebonne: the Amphitheatre

The Gallo-Roman theatre amphitheatre is the biggest and the best preserved theatre of its kind north of the Loire. Its size is exceptional.

Free visits. The key should be collected from the Cafe de l'Hôtel (closed on Thursdays).

### Saint Maurice d'Etalan: The Castle of Etelan

Built during the mediaeval period in an exceptional setting, the castle Etelan was reconstructed from 1494 onwards. The castle had several owners amongst whom figured Charles Henault, President of the Paris Parliament. During Henault's time, many philosophers were invited to the castle, including Voltaire. The style of the castle is flamboyant Gothic and its chapel is decorated with a baptismal font and statues.

The 16th-century paintings have been restored. From the park with its hundred-year-old trees is a view over to the valley of the Seine and the Brotonne forest.

The castle is open from 15 July to 31 August, daily with the exception of Tuesday, from 2.30 pm—6.30 pm. Group visits by appointment from Easter until All Saints' Day. Tel: 35 39 91 27.

## The Museum Victor Hugo at Villequier

The daughter of Victor Hugo, Leopoldine, and her husband Charles Vacquerie, were drowned in the Seine while boating in 1843. The death of his beloved daughter moved the poet profoundly and inspired him to write some of his most beautiful lines in the 'Contemplations' which brings visitors from all over the world to visit the house of the Vacquerie family built on the banks of the river. Numerous souvenirs recalling the friendship which united both the families Vacquerie and Hugo can be seen in this handsome, comfortable 19th-century house set in pleasant surroundings. Rare editions highlight the third national collection of drawings of Victor Hugo.

Open from 10am—12 pm and 2 pm—5.30pm (6.30 pm from 1 April to 30 September). Closed on Tuesdays (and on Mondays in winter). Entrance fee: groups at half-price. Paying guided visits on request. Groups by appointment. Tel: 35 56 78 31.

## The Church of Notre-Dame (Eglise Notre-Dame), Caudebec-en-Caux

In the pretty village of Caudebec-en-Caux the Church of Notre-Dame is a marvel of 15th-century late Gothic. The 54-metre tower built on the right flank has always been thought as one of the most beautiful of its kind in Normandy with the nave—especially on a sunny day—lit up through 16th-century stained glass.

## House of the Knights (Maison des Templiers) near Caudebec-en-Caux

The house, built in the 13th century, contains the Biochet-

Brechet museum collection of pre-historic artefacts and objects, as well as numerous drawings and engravings. There is an unusual display of more than a hundred old firebacks. Guided visit and, on request, an historic costume parade.

Open from 3 pm — 6 pm every day from June to September and during weekends in April, May and October. Open access. Groups by appointment. Tel: 35 96 00 21.

**The Seine Marine Museum near Caudebec-en-Caux**
This new museum, which is one of the amenities of the Ecomuseum of Lower Seine, is designed for the appreciation of the countryside, heritage and human activities of the maritime influence of the Seine. The boat shed houses among other things, the last 'gribane' of the Seine—a transport sailing ship until the beginning of the century. There are twelve permanent exhibitions and a well-explained trail passing several points of interest along the Seine.

Open from 15 March to 31 October 2 pm — 6.30 pm except Tuesday, but in July to August open on Tuesdays. In November and December: open at the weekend in the afternoon. Guided group visits by appointment. Entrance fee: groups at reduced rates. Tel: 35 96 27 30.

**The Abbey Saint-Wandrille, St Wandrille.**
The 7th-century Abbey of Fontenelle later took the name of its founder, Wandregesilus, an official of King Dagobert. Monastic life was interrupted several times, especially during the Viking invasions of the 10th century, but it revived and prospered in the Middle Ages until a decline in the 15th century. During the 17th and 18th centuries it was restored by the Benedictines of Saint-Maur who then sold it during the Revolution. Later, the writer, Maurice Maeterlinck, rented it for several years, then in 1931 the Benedictines returned having obtained relics of St Wandregesilus which had been in Belgium for 10 centuries. The ruins of the old abbey church (a mixture of 13th—14th century Norman and Ile-de France styles) can be visited all day. The 14th-century cloister and the present church (built from using the beams and stones of a 14th—15th century tithe barn moved from

another village in the Eure), are open to the congregation and to visitors at certain times when monks show you round.

Services: (gregorian chant) mass sung: Sundays and holidays, 10 am, weekdays 9.30 am. Vespers: Sundays and holidays: 5 pm, weekdays 5.30 pm, Thursday, 6.45 pm. Guided visits on Sundays and holidays: 11.30 am, 3 pm, 4 pm; weekdays: 3 pm and 4 pm (in the morning by arrangement). Entrance fee: groups, half-price. Tel: 35 96 23 11.

## The Abbey of Jumieges

The importance of these ruins is a reminder of the historical and economical role of the great abbey of the Vale de Seine, Founded in 654 by Saint Philbert, destroyed by the Norman invasions from 841 to 851, the abbey was reconstructed during the reign of William Long Sword, Duke of Normandy, around 925. The facade and the two bays of the Church of Saint-Peter, south of the great church, stem from the same period. The abbey church of Notre Dame was constructed from 1040 to 1067. The choir was reconstructed in the 12th century. Some early 12th-century elements of the chapter house and the cellars still remain. At the entrance to the abbey, the caretaker's house dating from the 14th century and the hostelry, much restored after 1863, still stand.

Open from 1 November to 31 March, weekdays 10 am – 12 pm and 2 pm – 4 pm; weekends 10 am – 1 pm and 2 pm – 5 pm except public holidays. From 2 April to 15 June and 15 September to 30 October, weekdays 9 am – 12 pm and 2 pm – 5 pm, weekends 9 am – 12.30 pm and 2 pm – 6 pm (except 1 May). From 15 June to 15 September, 9 am – 6.30 pm. Tel: 35 37 24 02.

## Church of Saint Valentin at Jumieges

The church was built by the monks in the 12th century. The nave with its large arcades date from the beginning of the 16th century. The choir with its ambulatory is an excellent example of gothic architecture.

## The Abbey Saint-Georges at Saint Martin de Boscherville

Raoul, who was chamberlain of William of Normandy,

founded a collegial in about 1050 on the ground where there had been several successive pagan temples followed by a chapel Saint-Georges built in the 7th century. The remains were unearthed by archeologists. Raoul set up regular canons in the chapel who were replaced in 1114 by Benedictine monks. The abbey church reconstructed next to the collegial strikes the visitor by the astonishing unity of its very pure Roman—Norman style as well as the very simple portal and the great aisle consisting of eight arches. There is a very beautiful apse with capitals recalling religious history one of which is the famous 'money dealer'. The 12th-century chapter-room is to be seen with its fully arched facade known for the quality of the sculpture on its historiated capitals.

Visits to the church are free. Exterior: Open from 1 April to 1 October, from 10 am—12 pm and 2.30 pm—6.30 pm. Closed on Tuesdays. Groups by appointment: 20% reduction for more than 30 persons. Tel: 35 32 01 32 or at the ATAR, Tel: 35 32 10 82.

### The Abbey Saint-Ouen in Rouen

Founded in the first half of the 6th century, the abbey, which later took its name from Saint-Ouen (archbishop of Rouen at the time of Dagobert), included a monastery until 1790. Today, only the great abbey church and the former dormitory from the 18th century (which became the Town Hall during the Revolution) remains, in a big, open square. The present church slightly larger than the cathedral, was built between 1318 and 1549 (the Hundred Years' War interrupted construction) and is a magnificent building where the unity of High Gothic can be seen at its best—exaggerating its proportions through a total lack of decoration but wonderfully light. The long nave is decorated with stained glass which leads on to the choir (1318—39), which also has 14th-century windows. The choir is closed off by an attractive 18th-century screen. The glass has been completed by the contemporary work of Max Ingrand. The windows mostly show the lives of saints. Above the transept crossing, is an 82-metre flamboyant spire crowned with an octagonal lantern. Recumbant figures of saints line the long Lady

Chapel in the apse. The great 1890 organ of Cavaille-Col, noted throughout France for its superior tone, is placed in an organ case of 1630. The facade, built in the 19th century, is somewhat dull except for the south side, which has a door with carved scenes from the Golden Legend, beneath the Porche des Marmousets.

The building is best seen standing back from the church to admire the apse and to best appreciate the central tower.

Open from 10 am — 5 pm daily from Palm Sunday to All Saints' Day as well as on Sundays throughout the year.

# CHAPTER TEN: HISTORICAL NORMANDY

**La route Normandie Vexin**
Running alongside the Autoroute de Normandie (A13) from Rouen to Paris the Seine curves through the pretty countryside following the 'Route Normandie-Vexin' a 120-mile tour starting on the N30 from Martainville to Vexin on the outskirts of Paris. The tour is based on 15 centres chosen for their historical interest, the rich architecture of the buildings, and the artistic treasures of both contemporary and former times.

Churches, mediaeval castles, sleepy villages and old farmhouses gave inspiration to the early impressionists and you can see why the canvasses of Claude Monet sparkled with the bright lights of leaf and flower. Starting at Rouen, the town itself is an impressive museum piece.

**Rouen 'Ville-musée'**
Magnificently situated on the banks of the Seine, the capital of Upper Normandy and fourth port of France possess splendid views. Its cathedral is one of the most beautiful Gothic buildings in France. The crypt, Lady Chapel and the tombs of the Dukes of Normandy, including Richard the Lionheart, can be visited on guided tours. Tel: 35 71 00 48.

The 'Gross Horloge' is a huge, colourful one-handed clock set in an arch. It was at one time on an adjacent belfry but in 1529 was repositioned over the street for ease of viewing. It is now convenient for photographs and every postcard of Rouen manages to include its image. Climbing up the many stone steps to one side, you have a wonderful view of the ancient houses and narrow streets and are level with a large bell cast in 1260 that rings the Conqueror's Curfew at nine o'clock each evening. Open April to September: 10 am – 12.25 pm and 2.30 – 5.30 pm. Closed Tuesday.

Other buildings to see are the Renaissance Palais de Justice, the church of Saint Maclou and the Church of Saint-Ouen, described in the Route of the Abbey (Chapter Nine).

Tourist Office: 25 place de la Cathédral. Tel: 35 71 41 77.

### Château de Martainville

Built between 1485 and 1510 by J L Pelletier, Marquis de Rouen, who wanted a residence in which to conduct his business. There is a Museum of Art with traditional crafts: a collection of furniture, glass, tapestries and agricultural machinery.

Open: every day except Tuesday and Wednesday and public holidays: 1 January, 1 May, 1 November, 11 November, 25 December. 10 am – 12.30 pm; 2 pm – 5 pm (winter); 10 am – 12.30 pm and 2 pm – 6 pm (summer). Guides on request: Tel: 35 23 44 70.

### Château de Vascoeuil. Museum Michelet

This privately owned stone castle with a red-roofed turret, is where Michelet wrote his History of France. A park of five hectares has a pretty waterfall. Important exhibitions of contemporary artists: Vasarely, Dali, Buffet, Trémois, L Fini, F Léger, Mathieu and Delvaux.

Open: from the end of March to mid-November every day 2.30 pm – 6.30 pm. Morning visits are possible for groups with an appointment. Tel: 35 23 62 35.

### Abbaye Cistercienne de Gontaine-Guérard

On the banks of the Andelle some 25 kms from Rouen is the delightful Abbey of Fontaine-Guérard. There are remains of the Abbey Church, the grand room, parlour, the work room for religious orders (in the primitive gothic) and the Chapel of St-Michel.

**Lyons-la-Forêt**
A classic site with its main town of Canton in the heart of the most beautiful countryside in France. There are 10,600 hectares in which to follow the pretty course of the Lieure, the small Cité de Lyons, and to enjoy the views. Tel: 32 49 31 65.

**Abbaye de Mortemer.**
This Cistercian abbey was founded in 1138 by Henry I of Beauclerc. Remains of the Church and the Cloister exist, plus a pigeon loft. There is museum of the monastic life; a son et lumière of the interior giving the life and legends of Mortemer. There are walks in the grounds and a small train route.

The park is open all the year round. Visit with commentary: the museum, with son et lumière inside, is open every day from 2 pm – 6.30 pm from Easter to 30 September.

**Château de Gisors**
One of the most beautiful examples of military architecture from the 12th century. The severe grey castle is surrounded by a high wall entered by a tall round arch. The central part of the interior has been transformed into a beautiful public garden. Visit the Governor's House, the Prisoner's Tower and also the caves.

Open from 1 April to 30 September every day except Tuesday from 10 am – 12 pm and 2pm – 6 pm. From 1 October to 1 April: only week-ends from 10 am – 12 pm and from 2 pm – 7 pm.

In the week, groups may visit on appointment: Tel: 32 27 30 14.

**Château de Boury.**
Built in 1685 from the plans of Jules Hardouin – Mansart, the privately owned Château de Boury is a perfect example of the classic French architecture in the province from the 17th century.

Guided tours: From Easter 15 October, Saturdays, Sundays and Holidays from 2.30 pm – 6.30 pm. Every day except Tuesday in July and August at the same times.

For group visits (minimum 25 people) in the week, write to: Château de Boury, 60240 Boury-en-Vexin. Tel: 32 55 15 10.

### Château d'Ambleville

Ambleville was built in the 16th century by Jean Grappin on the site of the church of Gisors. It was the home of Duplessy-Mornay, Counsellor of Gaspard de Coligny and of Henry IV.

Open: 15 May to 1 October Saturday and Sunday from 10.30 – 6.30 pm. Groups by appointment: tel: 34 67 71 76.

### Musée Archeological Departmental de Guiry-en-Vexin

20 kms north of Pointoise is the Archeological Museum of the Val-d'Oise. A total of 11 rooms present archeological objects of human work after the paleolithic age (300,000 years before Christ) until the Mérovingienne age (750 years AD).

Open in the week: 9 am – 12 pm and 1.30 pm – 5.30 pm (except Tuesday). On weekends and holidays: from 15 October to 14 March: From 1 pm – 6.30 pm; Summer: From 15 March to 14 October from 10 am – 12 pm and from 2 pm – 7 pm.

### Château-Gaillard Aux Andelys

A majestic fort of the 12th century built by Richard the Lionheart, King of England, Duke of Normandy. Constructed on a hill that dominates the Seine in the boucle des Andelys, Château-Gaillard is constructed as a major part of a vast system of defence which commands access to Normandy.

During the Religious War, after two years under siege, Henry IV ordered the Château to be destroyed.

Open: 15 March to 15 November every day except Tuesday, 9 am – 12 pm and from 2 pm – 6 pm. Guided tours: For groups, write or telephone Mme Momcomble, Mairie des Andelys, 27700 Les Andelys. Tel: 32 54 04 16.

**Château de Gaillon**
Situated on the highest dominant region of the Seine, a fortress between the royal domain and Normandy, the feudal manor was given to St Louis in 1262 by the Archduke of Rouen.

At present the building is undergoing extensive restoration and all visits are by request only to the Conservation Régionale des Monuments Historiques à Rouen, Tel: 35 63 40 36.

**Vernon**
The history of this town dates from the 10th century. The Church of Notre-Dame built in the 14th century is a remarkable example of Gothic art. Near to the Collegiale and in the other parts of the town are rows of houses dating from the 15th century, all restored to their original beauty. One of the most unusual buildings is the Musée Alphonse-George Poulain, 12 rue du Pont, which acts as a bridge.

Open: Every day except Monday and holidays from 2 pm—5.30 pm. The Collegiale has guide tours for groups: Requests to: Syndicat d'initiative, 36 rue Carnot, (face à la Mairie). Tel: 32 51 39 60.

**Château de Bizy (Vernon)**
This privately own château was constructed by Contant d'Ivry for Fouquet, Duke of Belle-Isle, Maréchal de France, about 1720. Baron de Schickler restored the Château and remodelled it on the style of an Italian palace, which is how it looks today.

Open: Every day except Friday from April to November, 10 am—12 pm and 2pm—6.30 pm. In July and August on Sunday: from 10 am—6.30 pm. Tel: 32 51 00 82.

**Giverny: Claude Monet: Maison et Jardins**
The Academie des Beaux Arts owns and manages the house and beautiful gardens at Giverny where Claude Monet embraced impressionism from 1883 until his death in 1926. The house is left as he furnished it, still with his Japanese prints on the walls. Although the gardens with the famous

Japanese bridge entwined with wisteria are always crowded, choose May or June for your unforgettable visit if you can.

Open: From April to November — house: from 10 am — 12 pm and 2 pm — 6 pm; garden: from 10am — 6pm (closed Monday). Write: Fondation Claude Monet, Giverny, 27620, Gasny. Tel: 32 51 28 21.

## ALTERNATIVE ROUTES
To help you plan a historic route, the Tourist Board has designed and mapped a number of recommended places of interest that are influenced by the lives of the Dukes of Normandy and of Brittany:

*Route 18: From Caen to Mont-Saint-Michel:*
Château de Fontaine-Henry
Château de Lantheuil
Château de Creully
Prieure de Saint-Gabriel
Château de Brecy
Abbaye de Mondaye
Château de Balleroy
Abbaye de Cerisy-La-Forêt
Château de Torigni-Sur-Vire
Abbaye de Hambye
Abbay de la Lucerne
Le Mont-Saint-Michel

For details, tel: 99 02 97 43.

*Route 19: Historic routes of the Dukes of Normandy:*

Château de Saint-Germain-de-Livet
Livarot-Saint-Michel de Livet
Saint-Pierre-Sur-Dives
Parcs et Jardins du Château de Canon
Château-Musée de Crevecoeur-En-Auge
Musée International du Mobilier Miniature et Château de Vendeuvre
Falaise

Parcs et Jardins du Château d'Harcourt
Château et Musées de Caen.
Honfleur

For details, tel: 31 89 23 30.

*Route 23: The Haras et des Châteaux de l'Orne:*
Haras du Pin
Château du Bourg-Saint-Leonard
Château de Medavy
Eglise d'Habloville
Château de Carrouges
Notre-Dame-Sur-L'Eau de Domfront
Château d'O
Saint-Germain d'Argentan
Château de Sassy
Chapelle de la Ferté-Mace
Abbaye de Lonlay
Cathedrale de Sées
Château de Flers

For details, tel: 33 27 20 83.

*Route 29: William the Conqueror (Guillaume-le-Conquerant)*
Bayeux
Lessay
Pirou
Domfront
Sainte-Suzanne
Le Mans
Moulineaux
Jumieges
Fécamp
Falaise
Caen

For details, tel: 43 01 40 10.

# CHAPTER ELEVEN: SAND, SEA AND D-DAY

In 1943, at the Quebec Conference towards the end of the second world war, the decision was taken to attempt a major landing operation on the European continent for Spring 1944; it was to be called Overlord. Contrary to the German command's expectation, it was not to be on the Northern coasts of France, near England, that the Allied Armies had decided to carry out their operation, but on the shore line of Seine Bay.

By landing on the beaches of Lower Normandy, which were less fortified than Pas-de-Calais, the Allies held the advantage of a surprise attack. As there was no big port in the area for unloading heavy equipment, they decided to construct two artificial ports, one opposite Arromanches, at the edge of the British sector, and the other opposite Saint-Laurent, in the American sector.

Just before the landing of the first troops, in order to confuse the enemy defence, the allied navy and air forces were to undertake a massive bombing of the Atlantic Wall fortifications. At the moment of attack, special armoured vehicles including amphibious tanks, bulldozer tanks and mine-clearance tanks, were to support the assailants.

**D-DAY**
The code name of 'Overlord' signified the colossal operation that was carried out under Generals Eisenhower and Montgomery as Supreme Commander of Allied Forces and

Commander-in-Chief of land forces. The landing operation began on D-Day (so-called because days A, B and C were judged to be not suitable) at dawn on the sixth of June by dropping three airborne divisions into the two front line flanks at Saint-Mère-L'Eglise and Benouville, the two extreme limits of the invasion front. Simultaneously, beach-heads were established in both the Anglo-Canadian sector (Arromanches-Courseulles-Ouistreham) and the American sector (Vierville-St-Laurent and Sainte-Marie-du-Mont), the former under the names of Gold, Juno and Sword Beaches, and the latter under those of Omaha Beach and Utah Beach. The parachutists' mission consisted of taking over certain key points—the artillery battery at Merville, the bridge on the Caen canal, roads and locks.

Shortly afterwards, a few hundred Rangers succeeded in capturing the fortified position at the Pointe-du-Hoc, and this was due to a particularly daring attack. At the same time, between 6.30 and 7.30 am, 120,000 men and about 20,000 vehicles were landing by sea on the five pre-selected beaches.

Even if the objectives for D-Day evening—Caen, Bayeux, Isigny, Carentan were not reached—on the whole the operation was a success. Except at Omaha Beach (Colleville-Saint-Laurent-Vierville) where the bridgehead continued to be rather weak despite the Americans' burst of courage, the losses were fewer than expected. It remained now to link up the five attacking beaches—Utah, Omaha, Gold, Juno and Sword—and to face the German counter attack.

## THE BATTLE OF NORMANDY (JULY – AUGUST 1944), CALVADOS

After joining up the five beaches and constituted a solid departure base 80 km long on the edge of the Channel, the Allies proceeded to carry out their plan. While the British concentrated their pressure towards Caen, attacking the German armoured divisions around this Lower Norman capital, the Americans set off from Utah towards Barneville in order to isolate the Cotentin peninsula. After the capture of the port of Cherbourg on 26 June, they opened a breakthrough towards the south in the direction of Coutances, Saint-Lô, Granville, Vire, and Avranches. To preclude any attempted counter-attack by the occupation forces, Montgomery, with the whole of the available Allied troops began a vast movement, encircling the German 7th Army which capitulated in the Falaise Valley. The allies had won their first victory on the continent. Three days later they crossed the Seine and entered Paris.

## LANDING SITES
Along the littoral of the Channel, between Ouistreham and Cherbourg, there are a series of monuments, steles and tables commemorating the exploits and sacrifices of the allied forces during the Overlord operation. In the sector of the British attack, between the Orne estuary and Arromanches, there are three exceptional sites: the German coastal artillery battery at Merville, captured by assault by a commando of parachutists of the 6th airborne division. Pegasus Bridge on the Caen canal to the sea captured by Major Howard's commandoes, and the vestiges of the artificial port at Arromanches (big concrete caissons marking off a vast road). Nearby, the marine artillery battery at Longues-sur-Mer is the only one on the Norman coast to have preserved its cannons. Further on, in the American landing sector, and beyond the beautiful Omaha beach, is La Pointe-du-Hoc, captured by the Rangers in a spectacular assault on the morning of the sixth of June, one of the important sights of interest in the circuit of Allied attack beaches.

## MILITARY CEMETERIES
### American cemetery
Situated on the summit of the plateau dominating the Omaha landing beach, the American cemetery of Volleville-Saint-Laurent stretches over 70 hectares, and was granted in perpetuity by France to the United States of America, in token of gratitude. In this vast rectangle which is set parallel to the coastline, and divided into ten squares, rest about 10,000 soldiers. The sight of the stark white crosses in hundreds of rows creates an awe-inspiring calmness. At

Saint-James, in the south of the Manche, is another US cemetery.

**Anglo-Canadian cemeteries**
In contrast to the Americans, the British have grouped their dead soldiers' tombs on Norman ground in many little cemeteries, scattered along the littoral. The principal ones are at Renville, at Bayeux, and at Banneville-la-Champagne, the smallest, at Brouay, Chouain, Fontenay-le-Pesnel, Ryes, Saint-Manvieu, Secqueville-en-Bessin, Tilly-sur-Seulles, Cames-en-Plaine, Douvres and Hermanville.

**Polish cemetery**
In the cemetery of Grainville-Langannerie, on the edge of the road from Caen to Falaise, the Polish soldiers killed in the Battle of Normandy are buried.

**German cemeteries**
About 75,000 German soldiers rest in Normandy in sombre graveyards. The biggest cemetery is at La Cambe (21,000 graves), a village between Bayeux and Isigny. The other cemeteries are situated in the Manche region at Orglandes, at Marigny and at Mont d'Huisne.

**MUSEUMS**
The number of museums about the second world war increases every year in France, especially in Normandy where they are more often known, not as 'war' but as 'peace' museums. New memorials and plaques are dedicated to divisions, regiments and some individuals who took part in the D-Day Landings and the Battle for Normandy. Museums are large and small; public and private. Some, like Hitler's Atlantic Wall defences, are well-preserved; the batteries at Longues and Crisbecq, for example, while shell holes still mark the landscape at Pointe du Hoc.

**Arromanches Landing Museum**
The permanent Landing exhibition is located in front of the remains of the extraordinary artificial port of Mulberry

Harbour. There are models, diorama, films. Open all the year, except from 1 to 22 January, from 9 am—11.30 am and 2 pm—5.30 pm during the high season from 9 am—6.30 pm.

**1944 Memorial Museum, Battle of Normandy, Boulevard Fabian Ware, Bayeux**
This retraces the military and human history of the Battle of Normandy, from 7 June to 22 August 1944. Open: from 16 March to 31 May and from 1 September to 15 October from 9.30 am—12.30 pm and from 2 pm—6.30 pm. In June, July and August, from 9 am—7 pm, without interruption, from 16 October to 15 March from 10 am—12.30 pm and from 2 pm—6 pm. For information: tel: 31 92 93 41.

**Museum of Airborne Troops, Bénouville**
The Pegasus Bridge' Museum retraces the historic hours of 'D-Day' (6 June 1944) and of the capture of Bénouville bridge. Open in March, April, May: from 9.30 am—12.30 pm and from 2 pm—6 pm; in June, September, October: from 9.30 am—12.30 am and from 2 pm—7 pm; in July and August from 9 am—7 pm. For information: tel: 31 44 62 54.

**Museum of the Poche de Falaise Battle, route de Bretagne, Chemin de Roches, Falaise.**
Open: every day from 10 am—12 am and from 2 pm—6 pm except on Monday and Tuesday. Every day in June, July and August. Closed from 1 December to 28 February. Tel: 31 90 37 19.

**Commando 4 Museum, placed Alfred Thomas, Ouistreham**
Tel: 31 96 63 10. Open on weekends from Easter to 31 May and in October from 9.30 am—5.30 pm, from 1 June to 30 September, 9 am—6 pm.

**Museum of Airborne Troops, Sainte-Mère-Eglise**
Tel: 33 41 41 35.

**Museum of the Battle of Tilly, Tilly-sur-Seulles**
Open: every day in June, July and August from 9 am—12

am and 2.30 pm — 7 pm and in September every day from 2 pm — 6 pm. Tel: 31 80 80 26.

**Omaha Museum, Vierville-sur-Mer**
Open: every day from April to September from 10 am — 12 am and from 2 pm — 7 pm. Tel: 31 22 43 66.

## MEMORIAL, A MUSEUM FOR PEACE, CAEN
An original idea, the Caen Memorial presents a journey through the history of our century, from 1918 until today. This trip through history is followed by three audiovisual shows which invite the visitor to reflect upon peace. A completely documented centre completes this museum which is unique of its kind in France. Opening hours: 15 January to 31 December, from 9 am — 7 pm; in June, July and August from 9 am — 10 pm. Tel: 31 06 06 44.

## VIN D'HONNEURS
Each year the Normans hold gatherings of 'Vin d'honneurs' which are friendly ceremonies for veterans and war widows. The fact that their liberation was won by huge civilian losses and the towns and villages were reduced to nothing does not lessen their warmth and appreciation at these reunions.

Good Fanco-American relations are still alive with continued remembrance of the events of June 1944. Not only veterans and widows visit the landing beaches but children interested in their family history and those from schools learning about where history was made.

Further information may be obtained from:

Comité Départemental du Tourisme du Calvados, place du Canada, 14000 Caen. Tel: 31 86 53 30.

Commonwealth War Graves Commission, rue Angèle Richard, 62217 Beaurains. Tel: 21 71 03 24.

American Cemetery Colleville-Saint-Laurent.
Tel: 21 71 03 24.

# CHAPTER TWELVE: ART AND CULTURAL THREADS

**BAYEAUX TAPESTRY**
Seventeen miles northwest of Caen, about fifteen minutes by car on the N13, is the home of a unique national exhibit, the Bayeux Tapestry at the Musée de la Tapisserie, Centre Guillaume le Conquérant, Rue de Nesmond, 14400 Bayeux. Tel: 31 92 05 48 and 31 92 13 37.

As the museum is in a one-way street running towards the cathedral from the east, you might find the easiest way to reach it by car is from the adjacent Rue aux Coqs.

The Museum is open daily from 16 March to 15 May and 16 September to 15 October, 9 am − 12.30 pm nd 2 pm − 6.30 pm. From 16 October to 15 March, 9.30 am − 12.30 pm and 2 pm − 6 pm (closed 25 December and 1 January). From 16 May to 15 September it is open 9am − 7 pm.

The ancient Bayeux Tapestry illustrates the story of King Harold and the conquest of England by William, Duke of Normandy, in 1066. It is superbly presented and you need at least two hours for a visit. There are documents, historical exhibits, a film and an audioguide tour (in six different languages).

On arrival, an introductory slide show is presented at 20-minute intervals with alternating commentaries in French and English. Slides are projected onto large sails of canvas hanging from the ceiling and representing a Viking long ship. In an adjoining room, you then walk along a photographic reproduction of the tapestry with explanations of the various scenes. Next, in a comfortable cinema, the scenes comes alive in a documentary film. When you reach the real Tapestry, displayed in a long, dimly lit room behind 30mm thick glass on a U-shaped stand, it is almost an anticlimax until your eyes become acclimatized and you can appreciate the exquisite detail of this historic work of art.

## Scenes of the tapestry

The brightly decorated material, 230ft 9in. (70.34m) long, 20 ins (50cm) wide, resembling an enormous 'comic strip', is an embroidery rather than a true tapestry. The design is stitched on rather than woven into what was probably unbleached linen. Eight colours can be distinguished against the now brown background—three shades of blue, one almost black, a bright and dark green, red, yellow or buff and dove grey. The colours appear to be chosen at random—a man's hair may be green, while a horse's body and near legs may be blue and the off legs red, with hooves of different colours.

The tapestry is divided into 72 scenes of mediaeval life, each with an embroidered title, separated from one another by trees or buildings. The large Arabic numbers 1 to 58 marked on the canvas outside the border were most likely added in the 18th or 19th centuries, possibly for the purpose of an exhibition.

Although sometimes referred to as the Tapestry of Queen Matilda (Tapisserie de la Reine Mathilde), wife of William the Conqueror, there was probably no connection with her. It is more likely, because he features in it so prominently, that the Tapestry was commissioned by Bishop Odo, William's half-brother, for the consecration of Bayeux Cathedral in 1077.

Originally of one length, experts cannot agree how many cuts and joins were made over the centuries, though the top border has an obvious additional strip of cloth, 8 in. (20 cm) of a slightly inferior quality added in parts. This frieze contains no figures but a decoration of blue stripes plus simple, double and triple crosses and various real and mythological creatures.

The border below the main scenes shows rural activities

including ploughing, harrowing, bird-scaring and hunting. There are also pictures from Aesop's Fables — evidence from other sources tell us that these were known by the 11th century — such as *The Fox and the Crow* and *The Wolf and the Lamb*. At one point, the Channel is so full of ships that the upper border disappears altogether and the lower border becomes part of the battlefield.

**The embroidery of the tapestry**
Although officially regarded as late 11th century, the date and origin has always been in doubt. The latest accusation about its authenticity has been raised by a British textile expert in Persian and European embroidery technique, Robert Chenciner: 'The thing that strikes you immediately is what superb condition it is in for a 900-year-old piece of fabric — much better shape than 15th- or 16th-century hangings.'

Chenciner's interest was first aroused in the scene of the feast where squares of meat are prepared on skewers. It was known that the Normans had knives with which to cut meat — indeed, there are knives in the Tapestry — but it was not known that they cut meat into cubes and skewered them like the Turkish shishkebab. In all other mediaeval records, meat was boned and jointed.

I discussed the situation at length with Mr Chenciner and examined published evidence. It appears that he no longer doubts the age of the linen, although carbon dating would date this more precisely, but the Keeper of the Bayeux Tapestry considers that to be 'unnecessary'. What he still believes, however, is that the draughtsmanship is of a poorer quality and inconsistent with other contemporary work and that the tapestry has been almost completely re-embroidered. His reasons are that it lacks the inked outline which is usually clearly visible on a work of that size and he has found signs of pin-pricks and tacking thread, both of which are common copying techniques. As there was no paper in the 11th century, the design would have had to be drawn onto the cloth for the embroiderers to work from. Mr Chenciner's argument is that although the linen cloth may have been washed during restoration, there should still remain the original cartoon outline.

Further discrepancies, he notes, lie in the style of drawing, with badly drawn folds of the hems of costumes, physical changes to the cloth, the history of the tapestry and, most of all, in the embroidery. It was surprising and untypical to use cheap woollen thread for embroidering such a monumental work—only gold or silk are found in other hangings. Also, judging from the colours, he maintains that one restorer used chemically dyed wool which was only introduced after 1865 (in contrast to 1842 which is given as the restoration date).

His is not the only opinion about the tapestry to annoy the citizens of Bayeaux—to whom after all it belongs. Others are that the embroidery was stitched by Anglo-Saxon nuns and that it was designed in England by book illustrators within twenty years of events depicted. Its English workmanship is explained by the appearance of an Anglo-Saxon letter among the capitals of the Latin text (AT not AD); different versions of William's name and repeated emphasis on Harold as King. For all this, the spelling can be attributed to a local Normandy dialect and despite any tenuous English connection, the tapestry was probably made by Norman workers at Bayeux.

Mr Chenciner has calculated that the hand-woven woollen thread would come from 50 sheep and that, despite its size, it need only have taken eight embroiderers ten working days to complete.

The method of embroidery was to cover the figures with worsted threads laid down flat side by side, then to bind them at intervals, knotting at the back. The seams, joints and folds were indicated by a type of twist. The faces and hands and, when bare, the legs, of people were outlined in red, green or blue, with yellow features, leaving for the skin colour the basic linen.

The tapestry contained 623 figures, of whom only four are women; 202 horses and mules; 55 dogs and 505 other animals; 37 buildings; 41 ships and boats and 49 trees—in all, 1,512 objects. The English have moustaches and long hair while the Normans are clean-shaven and have short hair.

## The storage of the tapestry

The first mention of the tapestry is an entry in the Bayeux Cathedral Inventory of 1476 where it is described as a very long and narrow strip or hanging (tente) of linen with embroidery using eight colours, of figures and inscriptions representing the Conquest of England. It was recorded as being carefully preserved in a strong wainscot press in a chapel on the south side of Bayeux Cathedral, and unrolled and hung round the nave, where it fitted exactly, once a year on the Feast of Relics, July 1, and throughout the following eight days. If in fact this happened every year for over six centuries the Tapestry would have been unrolled, hung up, taken down and re-rolled more than 600 times—probably would have been worn out.

The next record is of its 'rediscovery' by a French archaeologist M. Lancelot, who had been presented with a drawing of it and read a paper on the subject in 1724 without even knowing whether the 'sketch represents a bas-relief, sculpture, fresco, painting, or possibly a tapestry'.

Having heard of this document, a Benedictine of Saint-Maur, Father Montfacon, searched among his ecclesiastical contacts until he traced it to Bayeux. He then, in 1730, instructed a skillful draughtsman, Antoine Benoît, to copy the tapestry, but to alter nothing.

It became known in England when an antiquary, Dr Ducarel, described it in an appendix to his 'Anglo-Norman Antiquities', published with engravings, in 1767. From then on it was regarded in both countries as a monument of great importance.

In 1803 Bonaparte, as First Consul of France, had it taken to Paris for an exhibition at the national Musée Napoléon. When it was returned to Bayeux in 1804 it was stored at the Hôtel de Ville, 'coiled round a machine like that which lets down the bucks in a well'. Two years later it was reportedly being shown to visitors by unwinding it from one cylinder onto another.

The tapestry was properly exhibited for the first time at the Hôtel de Ville in 1842 after restoration of the damaged parts—particularly where it was very ragged at the end. During the first and second world wars the tapestry was kept in a number of places of safety until ending up at the Louvre, where it was placed on exhibition in November 1944.

## SCENES OF THE BAYEUX TAPESTRY
Any interpretation of the scenes of the tapestry would necessarily be long and speculative, but I list here, with brief notes, the expanded Latin titles as stitched onto the tapestry in Saxon manner. These, together with the excellent presentations at the museum about the rivalry between William and Harold and the conquest and final Norman victory, should guide you to fully appreciate this unique work of art.

**The story as it unfolds**

Harold attends the Court of King Edward the Confessor before his journey to Normandy.

Harold, called Duke of Wessex and Earl of Kent by contemporary historians, is a chief of the nation rather than the owner of a specific title. He rides to Bosham—a property of the Archbishop of Canterbury.

The Church at Bosham where he prays.

Harold sets sail and crosses the English Channel.

He lands on the coast of Pontheiu. In full costume, he nevertheless carries a spear, which seems to indicate he may be expecting an unpleasant welcome.

Guy, the Count of Pontheiu, seizes Harold and takes him prisoner: this was the custom at those times for any stranger arriving on the coast, even if shipwrecked.

Harold is taken in captivity to the Castle of Beaurain, capital of Ponthieu.

Harold and Guy converse about the reason for the visit.

Duke William's messengers come to explain their mission.

Turold: held by a historian to have been the designer of the tapestry who introduced his portrait here instead of in a more importance scene. He was, however, more likely to have been an important tenant of Bishop Odo who was sent as messenger of Duke William to secure the release of Harold.

Duke William's messengers.

Duke William of Normandy hears of Harold's capture.

Count Guy takes Harold to Rouen where he is received by Duke William at his palace.

A certain clerk and Aelfgyva. This is the most puzzling scene of the whole tapestry. This lady, with a Saxon name, is introduced here at the gate of William's palace with no reference to anything before or after.

Harold accompanies William's expedition against Conan, Earl of Brittany. They start for Mont-Saint-Michel.

They cross the River Couesnon at Mont-Saint-Michel. The river forms a boundary between Normandy and Brittany.

Harold rescues two men from quicksands. He heaves one man onto his back, while dragging another by the hand— probably impressing William with his physical strength.

Rennes: The Brittany campaign proceeds. Rennes was the capital of Brittany and the usual residence of Conan.

They come to Dol and Conan flees.

The castle of Dinan surrenders: Conan hands over the keys. There is some doubt about the translation of these last three towns and whether or not Duke William was actually fighting Conan or merely frightening him by entering the towns.

William knights Harold and they ride to Bayeux.

Harold made an oath to Duke William, calling a parliament in order to do so. The nature of the oath is not known but ranges from a promise to surrender the kingdom of England to William to a simple undertaking from Harold to marry one of his daughters.

Harold returns to England and is received by King Edward.

Edward's body is carried to the Church of St Peter the Apostle at Westminster where a sarcophagus was prepared to receive the royal corpse. The pictures now continue to substantiate the Norman claim by going back in time.

King Edward, in bed, speaks to his Council. He is in bed and receives his sorrowing friends. For seven days he was very ill but then he woke and described a vision. He said that the country would be cursed by God and harried with fire and sword. Then he said that he had promised many times to give his realm to the Duke of Normandy. He turned, not knowing what to do, and said he would consent to either the Duke or Harold as the barons please.

The King dies and is prepared for burial. Harold is elected and crowned King of England: everything happening in the space of forty-eight hours.

Archbishop Stigand is shown standing by the newly crowned monarch.

**The arrival of a star**
Men are dismayed at a star which they see as an omen. It

was on the ninth day of Easter and equal in size to a full moon. The appearance of Halley's comet as we now know it to be was noted in every chronicle of the day.

**Harold as King and William's reactions.**
King Harold is seated on his throne listening to a man standing at his right who may have been a messenger with news of the Duke's projected invasion.

An English ship carried the news of Edward's death and of Harold's succession,

News reaches William of Harold's Coronation while he was hunting in the park of Quevilly, near Rouen.

William orders that ships be built for the invasion of England.

Felling timber for ships.

Building the ships

They drag the ships to the sea.

They carry wine and arms.

Duke William and his army embark.

The invasion fleet crosses the English Channel.

William's ships approach the English Coast at Pevensey.

The Normans land and the horses are disembarked.

The knights push on to Hastings.

The knights seize cattle for food.

Wadard: a picture of a knight, (although there is no particular reason for his being here). Wadard is another form of a name for a warder of land—in this case, possibly a tenant of Bishop Odo.

**The cooking and feasting**
The meat is cooked and here the servants serve. Two cooks boil meat in a pot suspended between two forked sticks. The meal is cooked outside, the shishkebabs are made ready.

On English soil, the Normans feast. They eat round a convex table. The bundle of skewers in the servant's hand were possibly intended to be used to eat with, using a knife and fingers. Forks and spoons were not mentioned as eating implements until the 14th century.

**Preparations for war**
Bishop Odo, William and Robert: the three brothers hold a Council of War.

The Normans erect fortifications.

News of Harold and the movements of the English army brought to William.

The army leaves Hastings and goes out to battle.

The Norman army going to battle against Harold.

Duke William interrogates a mounted warrior named Vital if he has seen Harold's army.

Harold is told of William's army.

Duke William addresses his troops.

William's soldiers charge forth.

The Battle of Hastings.

The English army, drawn up in close ranks on foot, receives the Norman attack.

Harold's brothers, Leofwine and Gvrth are killed.

The battle rages. The Normans attack the English hilltop position.

Bishop Odo rallies the troops.

'Here is Duke William': the Duke refutes the rumours of his death.

He encourages his men, who begin to inflict grievous losses on Harold's army.

The death of King Harold.

The English continue to fight.

The French pursue.

The English flee the field.

**MUSEUMS**
National museums are closed on Tuesdays. Entrance fees average 15-30FF with a 50% reduction on Sunday. Young people under 18 are admitted free; 18–25 years old and persons over 65 are entitled to half-price tickets.

Municipal museums are closed on Mondays. The permanent collections are free and for their special exhibitions, visitors under 7 and over 65 are entitled to half-price tickets. Most museums are closed on Easter Sunday and Monday and Christmas Day and generally on public holidays.

**NATIONAL MUSEUMS AND EXHIBITIONS**
For a better understanding of the local traditions, some of the museums you should visit are listed below.

**Calvados**
Mining Museum at Le Molay-Littry
Farming Museum at Soumont-Saint-Quentin
Tools Museum at Pont-l'Eveque

**Eure**
Automobile Museum at Le Bec-Hellouin
19th century Folk Museum at Bernay
Textile Museum at Louviers

**Manche**
Cider making at Valognes
Farming at Ste Mère-l'Eglise
Copperware and furniture at Villedieux-les-Poles
Granite at St Michel-de-Montjoie

**Orne**
Sacre art at Sées
Folk traditions at St Cyr-la-Rosière

**Seine-Maritime**
Automobiles at Clères
Normandy folk art at Martainville

**Caen**
Musée des Beaux Arts,
Le Château, 14000 Caen. Tel: 31 85 28 63.

The museum is located in the heart of the city, in a park surrounded by the walls of the castle of William the Conqueror, which makes it an ideal visiting spot. The museum building, which opened in 1970 will soon be enlarged. Collections of faience work from Rouen, Nevers and Strasbourg, some goldwork, and paintings, principally 16th and 17th century Italian and Femlish, and 17th and 18th century French masters.

Open daily except Tuesdays and holidays: 10–12 noon and 1.30–5.30 pm 16 March to 30 September closes at 6 pm.

**Rouen**
Musée Le Secq Des Tournelles
Eglise Saint-Laurent, Rue Jacques-Villon, 76000 Rouen. Tel: 35 71 28 40.

The museum is named after Henri Le Secq des Tournelles (1854–1925), the donator of the most important collection of antique wrought iron work in the world. There are over 14,000 exhibits on all aspects of European wrought iron (except arms) from the Roman period until the Industrial Revolution, including locks of all types, signs, household utensils, tools and cutlery, as well as cultural and ritual objects, ornaments for costumes, writing implements and toilet articles.

Open daily except Tuesdays, Wednesday mornings and holidays: 10 am–12 noon and 2 pm–6 pm.

## ART IN THE EURE
Impressionist painters were very largely inspired by the landscapes of the River Seine. Monet, of course, was one of them, and his house still stands in Giverny. But Picasso, Lebourg, Sisley and Guillaumin, to mention but just a few, also scoured this valley for its many charms time and time again. More recently, Picasso stayed and worked for a time in Boisgeloup, near Gisors, and Bonnard chose Vernon. The little town of Conches was the birthplace and inspiration of François Decorchement, an acknowledged painter and master glass craftsman. Today, contemporary art is on display in the Château de Vascoeuil, the art centre at Jouy-sur-Eure and the museum in Evreux.

# CHAPTER THIRTEEN: MIXING BUSINESS WITH PLEASURE

The business centre of Normandy is found mostly in the Eure where medium-sized companies and subsidiaries operate in high-tech sectors such as pharmaceuticals, precision engineering, special metals and cars. Perfect illustrations are the SEP in Vernon, which builds engines for the Ariane space rockets, and CERDATO, the Atochem Research Centre sited in Serquigny near Bernay. There are Glaxo Pharmaceutical Laboratories at Evreux and Pasteur Vaccines at Val-de-Reuil.

Local authorities are planning the future industrial requirements of the countryside with great care. To improve life in these new zones, schools, universities, cultural and sports centres are being built and rapid communication systems constructed.

With the advent of the EC Single Market in 1992 there will be greater opportunities for the employment of experienced scientists, engineers and computer specialists in the area: the average age of the workforce is around twenty-two, many still being trained.

## WORKING HOLIDAYS

It is no easier in Normandy than in farming areas in other countries to find temporary work though there might be occasional apple picking and casual hotel work in coastal resorts. There is a demand for English teaching, but usually for a minimum of six months. 'Working Holidays 1991' is a comprehensive guide from the Central Bureau for Educational Visits & Exchanges, Seymour Mews House, Seymour Mews, London W1, tel: 071-486 5101.

## USEFUL BUSINESS ADDRESSES

Department of Trade and Industry, 1 Victoria Street, London, SW1. Tel: 071-215 7877; Tel: (French Desk); 071-215 4762; Fax: 071-215 5611. Jane Kirby will send you general information on exporting to France, with a list of publications, including a country profile, that may be purcashed or read in the DTI (Department of Trade and Industry) library.

French Institute, 17 Queensberry Place, London SW7 2DT. Tel: 071-589 6211; Fax: 071-581 5127.

French Trade Exhibitions: 2nd Floor, Knightsbridge House, 197 Knightsbridge, London, SW7 1RB. Tel: 071-221 3660; Fax: 071-792 3525.

French Consulate General (including Customs Dept) 21 Cromwell Road, London, SW7 2DQ. Tel: 071-581 5292; Fax: 071-823 8665. Telephone lines are always busy and the operators inclined to speak only French. I recommend you write or fax a letter instead.

French Embassy (Commercial Department), 21-24 Grosvenor Place, London, SW1 7JU. Tel: 071-235 7080; Fax: 071-235 8598.
The Commercial Department prefer you to telephone or write as their fax lines are very busy.

Food and Wine from France, Nuffield House, 41–46 Piccadilly, London W1V 9AJ. Tel: 071-439 8371; Fax: 071-434 9295.

French Centre: Chepstow Lodge, 61–69 Chepstow Place,

London, W2 4TR. Tel: 071-221 8134; Fax: 071-221 0642; Telex: 8950959 C FRANC. The Centre is a residence in central London with accommodation for 200 people in individual and multiple bedrooms. There are a number of meeting rooms, lounges and a restaurant. It is very convenient for business visitors from any country—rates from £20.70 per night. French Centre also organizes courses to improve your spoken and written French and runs a 16-week Saturday morning art appreciation course on 19th-century French painting. Special business packages and seminars can be arranged for individuals and groups.

## FRENCH CHAMBERS OF COMMERCE
French Chamber of Commerce: (Chambre de Commerce Française de Grande-Bretagne) Knightsbridge House, 197 Knightsbridge, London, SW7 1RB. Tel: 071-225 5250; Fax: 071-225 55 57; Telex 269132 FRACOM (Open 9am—1 pm). Any specific enquiry will be answered.

**Lower Normandy Regional Chamber**
Hôtel Consulaire, 41 boulevard Maréchal-Leclerc, 14037 Caen Cedex (Calvados). Tel: 31 85 18 68.

**Upper Normandy Regional Chamber**
Palaise des Consuls, quai de la Bourse, 76000 Rouen (S-Marit.) Tel: 35 88 40 42.

**Chamber of Commerce: Lower Normandy**
*Calvados*
14035 Caen Cedex: 41 boulevard Maréchal Leclerc. Tel: 31 85 49 68.
14600 Honfleur: 1, quai de la Tour. BP 136. Tel: 31 89 04 57.

*Manche*
50101 Cherbourg: 38 rue Francois-Lavieille, BP 106. Tel: 33 93 14 56.
50400 Granville: 14 rue Lecampion, BP 109. Tel: 33 50 05 35.

*Orne*
61002 Alonçon Cedex: 12 place du Palais, BP 42. Tel: 33 26 68 21.
61103 Flers Cedex: Aèrodrome Saint-Paul-la-Lande-Patry. Tel: 33 65 00 93.

**Chambers of Commerce: Upper Normandy**

*Seine-Maritime*
7621 Bolbec: 16 bis Avenue de Maréchal-Foch, BP 11. Tel: 35 31 00 78.
76202 Dieppe: 4 boulevard du Général de Gaulle, BP 62. Tel: 35 84 24 96.
76504 Elbeuf Cedex: 28 rue Henry, BP 465. Tel: 35 77 02 16.
76400 Fécamp: 2 place Beilet. BP 126. Tel: 35 28 00 99.
76067 Le Havre Cedex: place Jules-Ferry, BP 1410. Tel: 35 41 22 90.
76007 Rouen Cedex: Palais des Consuls. BP 641. Tel: 35 71 71 35.
Port autonome de Rouen: 34 boulevard de Bois-Guilbert 76037 Rouen Cedex: Tel: 35 88 81 56.
76470 Le Tréport: 2, quais de la République, BP 5. Tel: 35 86 27 67.

*Eure*
27001 Evreux Cedex: 35 rue Docteur-Oursel. BP 187. Tel: 32 38 21 61.

**BUSINESS EVENTS**
The Conference and Incentive Department of the French Government Tourist Office operates a venue-finding service, free of charge to meeting organisers looking for original venues in France. They will advise on business travel, seminars, conference, exhibitions and product launches. Tel: 071-629 1272; Fax: 071-493 6594.

P & O stockholders, besides up to 50% discounted return cross-Channel fare, there is also a discount voucher for the

Frequent Traveller annual cover. On their ferries, business travellers can pay a £7.50 supplement for Executive Club Class travel which allows the flexibility to cancel and rebook a sailing without incurring charges. The use of telephone, fax and photocopying facilities are available at extra cost on certain services.

# CHAPTER FOURTEEN:
# A PIECE OF NORMAN SOIL

With the increasing enthusiasm for buying homes in France, Normandy is one of the most popular places. Its ease of access from Britain and Ireland, a mild climate, and above all the friendliness and knowledge of English shown by the Normans, all go to make it a desirable part of the country in which to live. Buying a house in Normandy can be much easier than in England, and quite similar to that in Scotland. Once a decision is made and the buyer and seller agree, the rest of the formalities can be completed without waiting for searches, evaluations and mortgages.

While I don't want to discourage you, I think it would be prudent to understand as many aspects of house buying in France as you can. First of all not everyone is happy about foreigners purchasing property in their region, though those from Normandy are better than most. A few years ago I thought it was a brilliant entrepreneurial move to introduce British buyers to French estate agents who would arrange for a suitable selection of properties to be shown. The enterprise collapsed though before it got started because a female employee in the first and biggest agency with whom I'd set up my arrangement, sabotaged the communications. She tore up my letters, never put me through to the person I wanted to talk to and ignored all messages about times of arrival with prospective clients. I eventually managed to convey these problems to one of the directors and I understood the woman stopped working at the agency. In England, too, I had difficulty persuading French translators to deal with my correspondence. They did not want to help foreigners—even a friend—buy property in France. Luckily, the mood is changing but when assessing your future home, look also at the neighbours and their attitude towards you and your family.

**Finding your home**
Information about property for sale in an area of your choice may be obtained from estate agents in Normandy or possibly in the UK. Advertisements in specialized magazines or in the quality Sunday newspapers could point the way. The most successful, though time-consuming, method is to spend self-catering holidays, both in and out of season, in the type of property in which you are interested, getting addresses of those for sale from local people, the gîtes company, an estate agent, or a Notaire (Notary).

**The Notaire**
An indispensable person in any house transaciton in France is the Notaire. He (rarely a she) has the monopoly of conveyancing *(cession des biens immobiliers)* and he collects French taxes and acts as a representative of the government in authorizing all official documents.

He is also responsible for the payment of stamp duty and the 'droits d'enregistrement'—registration fees. He has to ensure that the deeds are correct, to make planning enquiries, and to be aware of any outstanding loans on the property.

Although the number of notaries is limited, as a house-buyer in a foreign country it would be ideal if you could find one who speaks English and understands the laws, not only of Normandy and France, but of the different parts of the UK too.

What is rather strange is that the Notaire can even act for both sides but this does lead to problems occasionally and you must remember that it is the buyer who has the choice of a Notary. The buyer pays all the notarial fees in the transaction, but if there are two notaries the fee is split between them.

You may be told that the seller's notary will be used as

he understands the local taxes and any potential difficulties but that might lead to more complications so do insist on appointing your own. The British Consulate, French or UK estate agents and banks might recommend a Notaire, or the local Chambers of Commerce are often most helpful.

A Notaire has considerable status and is given the title of 'Maître' with his office called an 'Etude', rather like a Judge in his Chambers.

**The contract**
When you have chosen your property you should be able to think about it before going ahead with the contract. Be very suspicious of those who want to force a sale through immediately. Don't sign anything without legal advice.

Although the actual process of buying a property is relatively easy, French law is complicated and all stages of a buying transaction and legal documents need to be explained in full.

You do not actually have to be in France at the time of completion but can appoint a person or company to be given Power of Attorney which can be signed at the French Consulate in the UK. It is recommended that someone acts on your behalf as documents may need to be signed at short notice.

**Estate agent (Agent immobilier)**
Most property or estate agents are members of the FNAIM (*Fédération Nationale des Agents Immobiliers*) which is the largest professional body in this field in France.

Some estate agents, as in any other country, are less honest than they should be, so even if you find one who speaks English, take care—even if you share the same nationality!

The seller usually pays an agent's commission, which is normally 5% but notaries can also be estate agents and take added commission so it is wise to understand the situation.

The French also avoid putting much in writing. They prefer face to face discussion (that's why cafes are so popular!), talking on the telephone—even overseas at great length and expense—and visiting people and places who have the right answers.

**Buying new property**
The common method of buying a new property—whether a house or a flat—is to buy *'en état futur d'achèvement'*—which is taken from a plan of the proposed building or complex. As in Britain, you are likely to get a better deal buying on the first phase when defects in building may occur through building on an unknown plot. It is important though to check for future stages of the development: houses built later may obstruct the view and change the surroundings significantly.

The sellers of new properties are likely to put more pressure on you to buy than an estate agent representing a small village houseowner but the law protects the buyer on these new properties. It also sets out the percentages of the total purchase price that have to be paid. However, the transfer duties *'droits de mutation'*, will be less than for an existing property although prices of new property are generally higher in the first instances as 'TVA' (VAT) may be due on the transaction.

You can often pay in stages and that is one of the advantages of buying new property—although the builders or developers may like more stages than are actually noted down in the contract. You may buy from someone who has bought a number of new 'plans' as a speculator, but you can still pay him in stages with his profit added.

**Buying a flat**
A flat has additional problems as it firstly will be *'en copropriété'*—a type of lease. You will have to assess the annual service charges; security arrangements; heating and air conditioning systems, etc.

Ask to see the previous owner's bills and if you can talk to them personally, so much the better. Try to find out who is responsible for major repairs such as those for the roof and any ground or garden maintenance.

## Survey of the property

The French do not have property surveyors as we know them and rarely survey a prospective property. It would, however, be wise to do so or at least make sure the structure appears sound by checking roofing, electrical wiring, dampness and so on.

## Bank accounts

Although it is not necessary to have a bank account in France, it is advantageous. When I was venturing into home ownership in France a few years ago neither English nor French banks were geared to help with mortgages, loans or advise on beneficial currency transactions. Now some banks of both countries in the large towns and cities are prepared to offer help.

Barclays Bank has just produced a book called 'Buying a Home in France' through their France Home Loans department and, for Barclays' customers in particular, it appears to be a useful service. The other big banks did not volunteer any information when I requested it and I could not find a British building society who had ventured into French property ownership loans, but that does not mean there aren't any.

## Inheritance laws and joint purchase

French inheritance laws apply to property situated in France, even if the buyers are not French nationals. Prospective purchasers are therefore strongly advised to seek legal advice concerning inheritance issues, especially when buying property as a joint purchase. The owner of the land is whoever is registered at the Bureau les Hypothèques and if the notary has registered the property incorrectly it may not revert to the survivor of the partnership.

## Taxes

House owners in France have two types of annual tax to pay:

1. 'Taxe Foncière' Land Tax payable to whoever is the owner of the property on 1 January of the fiscal year.

This is during the last quarter of the year.

2. 'Taxe d'Habitation' local rates: a tax covering services provided by the local commune. It is payable annually also in the last quarter of the year.

In the purchase of any old property a seller may want to be paid in cash to avoid paying the full amount of tax. Stamp duties are around 10% of the total price and the French have arranged an unofficial avoidance system of paying them in full.

The buyer pays an amount in cash for the promise of paying less stamp duty. The purchase is declared at the lower price and both the buyer and seller gain at the expense of the tax authorities—not only at the time of exchange but until the property is revalued.

The buyer is placed in a difficult situation because if he does not agree to this cash deal—which is illegal as he is likely to lose the sale. If he does agree and the tax authorities investigate the price, he may be liable for heavy tax penalties. They might decide to buy in the property at the declared contract price plus 10%. The buyer would then lose both the cash, if the seller did not return it, and the property.

### Import of household goods

When the final step has been taken and you are the proud owner of a Norman home, you will need to furnish it, most probably through the importation of personal and household effects. Full details of how to go about this are obtainable from the French Consulate General in London and there is different documentation for those who intend to live permanently in France and those with a second home.

In general, articles that have been in use for a period of at least three months may be admitted free of duty. These include furniture, household effects and personal belongings, including, for permanent residents, mobile homes, private vehicles, pleasure boats and private aeroplanes. New items and certain articles that don't qualify for relief of duty may, of course, still be imported but will be liable to TVA.

The most important documentation after a passport is, for permanent residents, either a contract of employment in France or a *'visa d'éstablissement'*, which is required (a) if you are an EC national not intending to work in France, or (b) a non-EC national. Applications for a visa should be made in writing to the Visa Section of the French Consulate General allowing a minimum of 22 weeks to get it.

Only a month is needed after completing a form sent to you from the Consulate to obtain permission to take personal effects in for a second home. You also have to prove the length of time you have lived at your British address—this could take the form of a letter from the Finance Office of a District council or a JP or a solicitor. Lastly, you will need two original copies of a detailed inventory in French, including vehicles, with a declaration that the articles are of the value stated and have been your property for the required number of months.

**French Customs (Douanes) in Normandy**
Le Havre: 201, boulevard de Strasbourg, BP 27, 76083 Le Havre. Tel: 35 41 214 34.
Rouen: 13, avenue de Mont-Riboudet, BP 4084, 76022 Rouen Cedex. Tel: 35 98 27 60.
Basse-Normandie: 44, quai Vendeuvre, BP 3101, 14018 Caen Cedex. Tel: 31 86 61 50.

**Pets and plant exportation**
Pets and plants are dealt with under the Ministry of Agriculture, Fisheries and Foods who will give you more information: Animal Health Division—Tel: 071-330 4411 and Plants Health Division (indicate the botanical name of the plants), Tel: 071-238 6483.

**Social security**
You may wish to secure continuity in the government social security scheme. For full information contact: Department of Health and Social Security, Overseas Branch, Newcastle-upon-Tyne, NE98 1YX.

**Driving licence**
For a driving licence you are allowed to drive in France on a British driving licence for no more than 12 months from the date of arrival, keeping an official translation in French of the licence at all times. After the first year you must hold a French driving licence and can apply for one at the local Préfecture who will tell you how to obtain one.

You will need to produce: (a) 'carte de sêjour' which will be issued to you once you are settled and (b) an official translation into French of your British driving licence.

## BECOMING A GITE OWNER IN NORMANDY
It is quite possible to own a gîte and manage it yourself but the Gîtes de France have introduced the possibility of becoming a gîte owner in Calvados or Manche with all the facilities and support of the Fédération Nationale des Gîtes de France for the promotion and letting arrangements. The owner may retain a certain number of weeks of residence for personal use.

The procedure is that the company sends you a list of properties for sale in Manche and a list of estate agents to be contacted in the Calvados area. Once you have chosen a specific property to buy, Gîtes de France will give you all the assistance you require. They also give grants towards the renovation and restoration of approved houses, taking into consideration the geographical position and condition of the inside and outside of the building.

While you are looking for a property to buy you may stay in a gîte. If you finally purchase a house and become a Gîtes de France owner 50% of the cost of your 'searching holiday' will be returned.

*Essential addresses*

Gîtes de France
178 Piccadilly, London W1V 9DB.
Tel: 071-493 3480 and 071-408 1343.
Fax: 071-495 6417; Telex: 89-52 059

Gîtes/Manche
Maison du Département
50008 Saint-Lô Cedex
Tel: 33 05 98 70.
Fax: 33 05 96 90; Telex: 772138F.

Gîtes/Calvados
6 Promenade Mme. de Sévigné
14050 CAEN Cedex
Tel: 31 70 25 25.
Fax: 31 70 25 70; Telex: 171300F

Other useful addresses

Centre d'Information des Notaires
12 avenue Victoria, 75001 Paris. Tel: 33 (1) 4233 7106.

Ordre des Architectes
140 avenue Victor Hugo 75116 Paris. Tel: 33 (1) 4563 9142.

British Embassy
35 rue de Faubourg Saint-Honoré 75008 Paris. Tel: 33 (1) 4266 9142.

For applications (in writing) for a mortgage contact:
Barclays Financements
Home Loans Unit, 5 rue du Cirque 75008 Paris.

## GLOSSARY OF COMMON PROPERTY TRANSACTION TERMS

*Acompte:* Deposit representing a certain percentage of the purchase price.

*Acte de ventre*: Deed of sale.

*Acte sous séin privé*: Private written agreement, not certified by a Notaire.

*Caisse de Caution Mutuelle:* Professional Indemnity Fund.

*Cession de biens immobiliers*: Conveyancing of property.

*Clause suspensive*: Let-out clauses figuring in most cases on the Preliminary Contract. The realization of such conditions is necessary to enable the completion of sale (e.g. obtaining a loan).

*Contract de réservation*: Reservation contract.

*Droits d'enregistrement*: Fees charged for registration of the contracts or deeds.

*Droits de mutation*: Transfer taxes,

*Etude:* The Notaire's office.

*FNAIM: Fédération Nationale des Agents Immobiliers*— National Association of Estate Agents.

*Frais de Notaire*: Notaire's fees.

*Multirisques habitation*: An insurance policy covering the building and its contents.

*Notaire:* Notary Public, given the title Maître.

*Offre préalable de crédit*: Preliminary loan offer.

*Plan de financement*: Financing scheme.

*Promesse de vente*: Preliminary Contract.

*SOCAF 'Société de Caution Mutuelle des Professions Immobilières et Foncières'*—a professions indemnity fund.

*VEFA 'Vente en Etat Futur d'achèvement'*—Purchase of a property still in its planning stage.

# CHAPTER FIFTEEN: TOWN TWINNING WITH THE UK

A twinning between two communities is a public statement of friendship and of intent to encourage goodwill between the two. As time goes by, Town Twinning means making opportunities for groups, large and small, individuals and families, to get together on each other's home ground and to entertain each other. It is hospitality that is freely given and equally freely received. The French word 'jumelage', denotes not only a natural twin whose relationship is not one of choice but also a 'blood brother' (one who swears mutual good faith deliberately), so the French put a great emphasis on their twinned counterparts.

Many towns in Normandy have twins in Britain to keep and develop friendships that often began in the war. The USA has two 'sister cities' in Normandy: Caen is linked with Alexandria, VA and Deauville with Lexington, KY. The twinning event itself may not conform to any set plan but it usually falls into a recognizable pattern. The major highlight is likely to be a dinner, at which everyone can get together in a convivial atmosphere; a speech or two, a charter which sums it all up in somple terms and is signed by representatives from both communities; then a symbol of the future together, such as the planting of a tree. Twinning can involve schoolchildren, philatelists, footballers, hockey players, cyclists, athletes, dancers, police officers, fire fighters and town and district officials—in fact anyone.

Co-incidentally, town twinning began with two places in Britain and France: when in 1919 the Mayor of Blackburn, visited Péonne in the Somme region. His son had died there, in a world war battery on the River Somme. Partly as a reaction to the uselessness of war, partly in response to the friendliness of the local French people, the mayor decided to help rebuild the town. Once back in Blackburn, he persuaded citizens to contribute to the cost of a new bridge in Péonne. It was a small but symbolic bridge.

The idea of twinning was revived in 1942 when Coventry contacted Stalingrad (now Volgograd) in Russia after it had been badly bombed. Coventry had suffered a similar experience and wanted to show that peace could now be taken for granted.

The *département* of Calvados has developed its closeness with Devon. Not only are the two counties twinned but almost every town in each place has a twin across the channel. The *département* of Orne too is twinned with Somerset and those counties also have many town links.

For details of finding Norman partners, David Herbert is the Twinning Officer at the Local Government International Bureau, 35 Great Smith Street London, SW1P 3BJ. Tel: 071-222 1636; Fax: 071-233 2179. The total number of twinnings is now over 1500 and between 50 and 60 are added each year!

**Cultural Exchanges**
Some towns don't have a formal link but, as in the case of Brighton and Dieppe, they historically have much in common and have developed friendly official exchanges, particularly in art and culture. A festival chorus from Brighton took a specially commissioned oratorio to Dieppe's arts venue — the *Centre d'Action Culturelle Jean-Renoir* (the CAC) — while in return *La Tempesta di Mare* — nine Dieppe-based musicians — played Baroque music on original instruments in Brighton's Royal Pavilion Music Room.

Sometimes artistic links take an unexpected turn. As an example, a resident of Arque-la-Bataille, five miles from Dieppe, was sure there was a Turner landscape featuring the town's ruined hilltop castle. A Brighton journalist, Peter Avis, who fosters the Brighton-Dieppe friendship, heard about this and after much research uncovered the almost forgotten picture—in the vaults of Brighton Museum! Thanks to Brighton's Museums Department a reproduction now hangs on a wall in Arques.

However, twinning cannot be held responsible for individual actions. I heard that a Devon teacher arranged a year's exchange with a twinned school in Calvados then decided he wanted to stay there permanently. He returned to his small town only to give in his notice and tell his wife he was leaving her!

## NORMANDY VILLAGES, TOWNS AND CITIES AND THEIR BRITISH TWINS

**Eure**
Beaumont-le-Roger—Wotton-under Edge, Gloucestershire
Bernay—Haslemere, Surrey
Brionne—Shaftesbury, Dorset
Conches—Wareham, Dorset
Cormeilles—Chepstow, Gwent, Wales
Evreux—Rugby, Warwickshire
Gasny—Castle Donnington, Leicestershire
Le Neubourg—Gillingham, Dorset
Louviers—Weymouth & Melcombe Regis, Dorset
Muids—Norton, Suffolk
Nonancourt—Ringwood, Hampshire
Verneuil-sur-Avre—Stowmarket, Suffolk

**Seine Maritime**
Bihorel—Stoke Golding, Leicestershire
Caudebeck-en-Caux—Uppingham, Leicestershire
Deville-Les-Rouen—Syston, Leicestershire
Dieppe—Melton Mowbray, Leicestershire
Fécamp—Vale of Glamorgan, South Galmorgan. Wales
Fleury-sure-Andelle—East Goscote, Leicestershire
Grand Quevilly—Hinley, Leicestershire
La Bouille—Whitchurch, Oxfordshire

Le Frenaye—South Wonston, Oxfordshire
La Havre—Southampton, Hampshire
Lillebonne—Wellington, Somerset
Malaunay—Sandy, Bedfordshire
Maromme—Oadby and Wigston, Leicestershire
Mont St Aignan—Edenbridge, Kent
Neufchatel-en-Bray—Whitchurch, Shropshire
Notre Dame-de-Gravenchon—Street, Somerset
Offranville—Thurmaston, Leicestershire
Petit-Couronne—Beccles, Suffolk
Plateau est la Rouen—Bradgate Villages, Leicestershire
Plateau Nord de Rouen—Kegworth, Leicestershire
Quincy Voisini—Braunston, Northamptonshire
Rouen—Norwich, Norfolk
St Etienne-du-Rouvray—Felling, Tyne & Wear
St Valéry en Caus—Inverness, Highlands
Veullettes—Greenock, Strathclyde, Scotland
Yvetot—Lanark, Strathclyde, Scotland

**Calvados**
Amfreville—Dolton, Devon
Arromanches—Instow, Devon
Asnelles—Charmouth, Dorset
Aubigny—Stoke Mandeville, Buckinghamshire
Aunay-sur-Odon—Holsworth, Devon
Balleroy—Shebbear, Devon
Bavent—Stoke Canon, Devon
Bayeux—Dorchester, Dorset
Beauville-Bieville—Lympstone, Devon
Beuvron-en-Auge—Woolsery, Devon
Blangy-le-Château—North Tawton, Devon
Bonnebosq—Cheriton Fitzpaine, Devon
Bretteville-sur-Laize—Chagford, Devon
Bretteville-sur-Odon—Woodbury, Devon
Cabourg—Salcombe, Devon
Caen—Coventry, West Midlands and Portsmouth, Hampshire
Cahagnes—Horsted Keynes, West Sussex
Cambremer—Witheridge, Devon

Canteloup-Cléville—Ide, Devon
Caumont L'Evente—Uffculme, Devon
Cesny Bois Halbout—Clovelly, Devon
Clécy—Ermington, Devon
Colombelles—Fremington, Devon
Cormelles-le-Royal—Combe Martin, Devon
Cormolain—Burrington, Devon
Courseulles-sur-Mer—Dartmouth, Devon
Crèvecoeur-en-Aug—Newton Poppleford, Devon
Crouay—Braishfield, Hampshirre
Deauville—Cowes, Isle of Wight
Démouville—Sandford, Devon
Dozulé—Leonard Stanley, Gloucestershire
Falaise—Henley-on-Thames, Oxfordshire
Fontaine Henry—Scorriton, Devon
Fontenay-le-Marmion—Chulmleigh, Devon
Grainville-Langannerie—Lapford, Devon
Honfleur—Sandwich, Kent
Houlgate—Axbridge, Somerset
Isigny-sur-Mer—Kingsbridge, Devon
Le Molary-Littry—Bovey Tracey, Devon
Lisieux—Taunton, Somerset
Liverot—South Molton, Devon
Mathieu—Burrator, Devon
Merville-Franceville-Plage—Clyst St Mary, Devon
Mery Corbon—Mary Tavy, Devon
Mézidon—Honiton, Devon
Mondeville—Northam, Devon
Nonant—Bratton Clovelly, Devon
Orbec—Kingsteignton, Devon
Osmanville—Combinteignhead, Devon
Ouistreham-riva-Bella—Angmering, West Sussex
Petiville—Lydford, Devon
Pont d'Ouilly—Chipping Campden, Gloucestershire
Pont L'Eveque—Ottery St Mary, Devon
Rosel—Goodleigh, Devon
Rots—Newton St Cyres, Devon
St Cyr du Ronceray—Copplestone, Devon
St Gatien-des-Bois—Morchard Bishop, Devon

St Honorine-due-Fay—Swimbridge, Devon
St Martin-des-Besaces—Slaugham, West Sussex
St Martin-de-Bienfaite—Bow, Devon
St Martin-de-Mailloc—Chawleigh, Devon
St Martin-de-Sallen—Bratton Fleming, Devon
St Pierre-sur-Dives—Ivybridge, Devon
St Vaast-sur-Seulles—Bridford, Devon
St Vigor-le-Grand—Coldon common, Hampshire
Sannerville—Exminster, Devon
Sept Vents—Poughill, Devon
Sequeville-en-Bessin—Farringdon, Devon
Soliers—Ipplepen, Devon
Thury Harcourt—Seaton, Devon
tilly-sur-Seulles—Horrabridge, Devon
Touques—Speyside, Grampian
Treviers—Stokeinteignhead, Devon
Troarn—Chudleigh, Devon
Trouville—Barnstaple, Devon
Venoix—Livermead & Cockington, Devon
Vieux—Otterton, Devon
Villers-Bocage—Bampton, Devon
Villiers-sur-Mer—Wickham, Hampshire
Vire—Totnes, Devon

**Manche**
Briquebec—Alresford, Hampshire
Carentan—Selby, North Yorkshire
Cherbourg—Poole, Dorset
Coutances—Ilkley, West Yorkshire
Gavray—Launton, Oxfordshire
Hambye—Lacey Green, Buckinghamshire
Lessay—Boxgrove, West Sussex
St James—Beaminster, Dorset
St Lô—Christchurch, Dorset
St Sebastien du Raids—Bradford Peverell, Dorset
St Vasst-la-Hougue—Bridport, Dorset
Torigni-sur-Vire—Shipston-on-Stour, Warwickshire
Valognes—Wimborne Minster, Dorset

**Orne**
Alençon—Basingstoke, Hampshire
Argentan—Abingdon, Oxfordshire
Athis-de-L'Orne—Bromyard, Hereford and Worcester
Bellême—Goring, Oxfordshire
Flers—Warminster, Wiltshire
Gacé—Kinross
La Ferté Macé—Ludlow, Shropshire
Longny au Perche—Milverton, Somerset
Lonlay L'Abbaye—Stogursey, Somerset
Remalard—Castle Cary
Sées—Southwell, Nottinghamshire
Vimoutiers—Fordingbridge, Hampshire

# APPENDIX I

## A LIST OF ALL PLACES IN NORMANDY WITH AT LEAST ONE HOTEL

Acquigny
Agneaux
Agon-Coutainville
L'Aigle
Alencon
Amfreville
Les Andelys
Annebault
Antoigny
Argentan
Arromanches-Les-Bains
Audrieu
Aumale
Aunay/Odon
Avranches
Bagnoles-de-L'Orne
Balisne
Barentin
Barfleur
Barneville-Carteret
Barneville-La-Bertran
Bavent
Bayeyx
Bazincourt/Epte
Beaubray
Beaumont-Le-Roger
Beauvoir
Bec-Hellouin
Bellefontaine
Bellême
Benouville
Bernay
Berneval/Mer
Beuzeville
Bezancourt
Blonville-Sur-Mer
Bois-Guillaume
Bolbec
Bonsecours
La Bouille
Bourg-Saint-Léonard
Bourgtheroulde
Bréhal
Breteuil/Iton
Le Breuil-En-Bessin
Bréville/Mer
Bricquebec
Brionne
Briouze
Brix
Cabourg

Caen
Cailly-Sur-Eure
Calleville
Campigny
Canapville
Canisy
Carentan
Carrouges
Caudebec-en-Caux
Caumont/Orne
Ceaux
Cerences
Cerisy-La-Salle
La Chapelle d'Andaine
Charleval
Chateau/Epte
Chef-du-Pont
Cherbourg
Clecy
Cléon
Colombelles
Commes
Conches-en-Ouche
Condé/Noireau
Condeau
Cormeilles
Corneville-sur-Risle
Coudeville
Coulonges-les-Sablons
Courgeoust
Courseulles/Mer
Courtils
Coutances
Couterne
Creully
Croixmare
Damville
Deauville
Dieppe
Dives-sur-Mer
Domfront
Donville-les-Bains
Douains
Dozule
Drubec
Ducey
Duclair
Ecouché
Elbeuf
Equeurdreville
Esclavelles
Etrépagny
Etretat
Eu
Evreux
Falaise
Fauville-en-Caux
Fécamp
La Ferrière-aux-Étangs
La Ferrière/Risle
Ferruières-en-Bray
La Ferté-Frésnel
La Ferté-Macé
Fervaques
Flamanville
Flers
Fleury/Andelle
Fontenai-sur-Orne
Forges
Forges-Les-Eaux
Franqueville-Saint-Pierre
Gacé
Gieville
Gisors
Giverny
Fongreville-L'Orcher
Goupillières
Gournay-en-Bray

Le Grand-Quevilly
Grandcamp-Maisy
Grandchain
Les Grandes-Ventes
Granville
Hambye
Harfleur
Hauteville/Mer
Hautot/Mer
Le Havre
La Haye-du-Puits
La Haye-Pesnel
Héricourt-en-Caux
Hermanville/Mer
Hérouville-Saint-Clair
Honfleur
Houlgate
Illiers-L'Evéque
Isigny/Mer
Ivry-La-Bataille
Jullouville
Juvigny-sous-Andaine
La Lacelle
Langrune/Mer
Lessay
Lieurey
Lillebonne
Lion/Mer
Lisieux
Livarot
Londinières
Longny-au-Perche
Louvetot
Louviers
Luc/Mer
Lyons-La-Forêt
Macé
La Mailleraye/Seine
Martin-Egise

Le Mêle-sur-Sarthe
Menesqueville
Le Merlerault
Merville-Franceville
Les Mesnil-Esnard
Mesnil-Val
Meulles
Le Molay-Littry
Mondeville
Mont-Saint-Aignan
Le Mont-Saint-Michel
Montebourg
Montfort-Sur-Risle
Montigny
Montivilliers
Montmartin-en-Graignes
Montmartin/Mer
Montpinchon
Mortagne-au-Perche
Mortain
Moulins-la-Marche
Mutrecy
Le Neubourg
Le Neufbourg
Neufchatel-en-Bray
Neuvy-au-Houlme
Nonancourt
Nonant
Nonant-le-Pin
Norville
Notre-Dame-de-Bondeville
Notre-Dame-de-Courson
Noyers-Bocage
Orbec
Oistréham-Riva-Bella
Pacy-Sur-Eure
Passais-la-Conception
Perriers

Le Petit-Couronne
Le Petit-Quevilly
Lers Petites Dalles
Pirou
Pont-Audemer
Pont d'Ouilly
Pont-L'Evéque
Pont-Saint-Pierre
Pontaubault
Pontorson
Port-en-Bessin
Portbail
Potigny
Putanges-pont-Ecrepin
Quettehou
Quetteville
Quettreville/sienne
Quiberville/Mer
Quillebeuf-sur-Seine
Quineville
Rânes
Ranville
Rémalard
Reville
La Rivière-Thibouville
Rosay-sur-Lieure
Rouen
Rouxmesnil-Bouteilles
Rugles
Sahurs
Saint-Adrien
Saint-Aignan-de-Cramesnil
Saint-André/Cailly
Saint-André-d'Herbertot
Saint-Aubin-le-Vertueux
Saint-Aubin/Mer
Saint-Benoist-des-Ombres
Saint-Denis-sur-Sarthon

Saint-Etienne-du Rouvray
Saint-Gatien-des-Bois
Saint-Georges-du-Vièvre
Saint-Germain-des-Vaux
Saint-Gauburge
Saint-Hilaire-du-Harcouet
Saint-James
Saint-Jean-le-Thomas
Saint-Joseph
Saint-Léonard
Saint-Lô
Saint-Marcel
Saint-Martin-aux-Chartrains
Saint-Martin-des-Champs
Saint-Martin-du-Vivier
Saint-Michel-des-Anaines
Saint-Pair-sur-Mer
Saint-Pierre-de-Bailleul
Saint-Pierre-des-Fleurs
Saint-Pierre/Dives
Saint-Pierre-du-Vauvray
Saint-Pierre-la-Rivière
Saint-Quentin-sur-le-Homme
Saint-Sauveur-le-Vicomte
Saint-Sever
Saint-Vaast-La-Hougue
Saint-Valéry-en-Caux
Saint-Vigor-le-Grand
Sainte Gauburge
Sainte-Adresse
Sainte-Cécile
Sainte-Marguerite/Mer
Sassetot-le-Mauconduit
Sées
Siouville-Hague
Sotteville-Les-Rouen
Sotteville/Mer

Tancarville
Tanis
Le Teilleul
Tessé-la-Madeleine
Tessy/Vire
Thury-Harcourt
Tillières/Avre
Tilly/Seulles
Tinchebray
Torigni/Vire
Tourgeville
Tourlaville
Tourouvre
Tourville-la-Rivière
Tracy-sur-Mer
Le Trait
Trelly
Le Tréport
Troarn
Trouville/Mewr
Urville-Nacqueville
Val-de-Reuil
Valmont
Valognes
Varengeville/Mer
Le Vaudreuil
Vendeuvre
Ver/Mer
Verneuil/Avre
Vernon

Veulettes/Mer
Vierville/Mer
Vieux-Villez
Villedieu-les-Poeles
Villers-Bocage
Villers/Mer
Villerville/Mer
Vimoutiers
Vire
Vironvay

ALSO AVAILABLE FROM ROSTERS

TALKING TURKEY by Alison Rice (£5.95)

A lively and entertaining look at this newest holiday sensation. Travel writer and broadcaster Alison Rice has produced an up-to-date guide to the main Turkish resorts and Istanbul. Aimed at visitors new to Turkey it explains what to see, where to stay — and equally important, what to avoid. Includes basic Turkish phrases plus hints on making the best of the food, wine and shopping available.

VIVA ESPANA by Edmund Swinglehurst (£5.95)

Discover the real Spain before the bulldozers and industrialists have destroyed its natural beauty. In this comprehensive guide to Spain, Edmund Swinglehurst, travel expert and author, has provided a fascinating glimpse behind the veil of Spain to show you the heart of the countryside, its people, its culture and its way of life.

CHAMPAGNE ON A BUDGET by Patrick Delaforce (£5.95)

Champagne is probably the world's most famous wine — yet few people have discovered the sparkling region where it is produced. Wine expert and travel writer Patrick Delaforce shows you how to enjoy a trip to the Champagne region, suggests tours, visits to vineyards and gives advice on the wines worth sampling. Aimed at the independent traveller who does not wish to bust his budget this book includes lists of medium priced hotels and restaurants plus handy hints on enjoying your stay.

FRENCH RIVIERA ON A BUDGET by Patrick Delaforce (£5.95)

The land of celebrities, champagne cocktails and caviare is just waiting to be discovered. In this timely guide travel writer Patrick Delaforce shows that you don't need to break the Bank at Monte Carlo to enjoy a stay among the rich and famous along the world's famous Cote d'Azur. He lists medium priced hotels, restaurants plus plenty of advice on how to spend those sun filled days and fun filled nights.

BURGUNDY AND BEAUJOLAIS ON A BUDGET by Patrick Delaforce (£5.95)

Discover one of France's most beautiful wine regions without spending a fortune. Patrick Delaforce, wine expert and travel writer, reveals the true heart of the French countryside. Just one hour's drive from Paris lies Burgundy, famous the world over for its wines, but also one of the most beautiful and intriguing regions in France. For the gourmet there is the chance to visit the vineyards where Chablis and Beaujolais are made and sample local produce such as truffles, river fish, fine game and fresh fruits. Includes: regional tours, local wines and wine co-operatives, value for money accommodation and restaurants, places of interest, regional events.

GASCONY AND ARMAGNAC ON A BUDGET by Patrick Delaforce (£5.95)

Discover one of France's best kept secrets — the land of brandy, beaches and Basque cuisine. Wine expert and travel writer Patrick Delaforce reveals the heart of one of France's most inviting holiday locations. From the beautiful silver coast fringed with pine forests through to the inland villages, there is an alluring countryside just waiting to be discovered. Magnificent beaches, sophisticated nightlife and superb cuisine. Includes: regional tours, local wines and wine co-operatives, value for money hotels and restaurants, places of interest and regional events.

IS IT WORTH ANYTHING? by Stephen Ellis (£3.99)

Most of us have drawers filled with odds and ends. But are they worth anything? Stephen Ellis writes on the money pages of the Daily Mirror which gets thousands of letters from readers asking just that. So here for everyone who cannot bear to throw anything away 'just in case' is the book which will give most of the answers. Includes: toys, stamps, glass, jewellery, postcards, records and much more.

COOK AND HOUSEWIFE'S MANUAL by Mistress Margaret Dods (hardback £14.95)

With an introduction by Glynn Christian

Discover the world of Mistress Margaret Dods and the Cleikum Club. Mistress Dods was the founder of one of the first cookery clubs in the country and her manual, first published in 1829, includes the story of how the club was set up, over 1,000 recipes as well as hints on wine making, curing meats and making cheese. Glynn Christian says 'It is a real cookery book, a book for people who really like to eat. Comic and revelatory'. Recommended by Chat and the Glasgow Herald.

NEW FEMALE INSTRUCTOR (hardback £12.50)

First published in the 1830's the book was designed to be a practical manual aimed at turning every one of its fair readers into an intelligent and pleasing companion. It includes: dress, fashion, morals, love, courtship, duties of the married state, conduct to servants plus more than 100 pages of recipes. Lively, entertaining — the perfect gift.

THE SHARE BOOK (3rd ed) by Rosemary Burr (£5.99)

With an introduction by the Rt. Hon. Mrs. Margaret Thatcher

An up-to-date, completely revised edition of this bestselling guide to the stockmarket which has been bought by more than 50,000 people. Includes advice on every aspect of buying, selling and choosing shares. A full glossary, details of members of the Stock Exchange, Unit Trust Association and Association of Investment Trust Companies. Plus new rules on investor protection and unit trust pricing. The classic companion for anyone interested in stocks and shares.

YOUR BUSINESS IN 1992 by James Dewhurst (£6.95)

Chartered accountant, author and authority on business management, James Dewhurst has distilled his experience into this valuable addition to any businessman's library. What will the much heralded internal market in Europe mean in pratice to you and your business? The answers are inside. Includes: setting common standards, enforcing technical requirements, competing for orders from public bodies, distribution services, prospects for take-overs and mergers, new tax environment and much more.

HOMEOWNERS SURVIVAL GUIDE ed. Rosemary Burr (£3.95)

Recommended by the Financial Times, the Sun and the Times. Everything the homeowner needs to make the most of his or her investment and run their home cost effectively. Includes: choosing your home, arranging the finance, countdown to purchase, insurance, decoration, home improvement moving on and cost cutting ideas.